HEAR THE SPIRIT

ISBN: 0-9673416-9-8

Published in the United States by the Baptist World Alliance
405 North Washington Street, Falls Church, Virginia, 22046

HEAR THE SPIRIT

The Official Report of the Twentieth Baptist World Congress
Honolulu, Hawai'i, July 28-August 1, 2010

Edited by Neville Callam

Table of Contents

PART III Congress Program

PART IV   Congress Information

PART V BWA Information

Appendices

Preface

Many of those who made their way from Honolulu, Hawai`i, at the end of the 20th Baptist World Congress, agreed that they had just benefitted from what was a mountain top experience. Writing in the immediate aftermath of the event, for the sake of this publication, it is easy to overestimate the impact of the event.

Congress 2010 was a time of rich fellowship. The opportunity for thousands of Baptists to meet in a single venue is a treasured one. The gathering and mingling of people from many different backgrounds and cultures who are bound together by a common commitment to Jesus Christ is a special privilege and Honolulu provided a great context for this rich time of fellowship and sharing.

Congress 2010 was a time of inspiration. It was a great feast of preaching and teaching. Two major sessions each day featured spiritual reflections that were offered by women and men representing the six different regions of the Baptist World Alliance. This provided a variety of insights developed in different contexts and supplying a fare that, even in an age of multi-cultural societies, a single context can hardly offer.

Congress 2010 was a time of singing. Choirs and singers from around the world offered up their gifts to the Lord and raised a memorable paean reflecting the joy of Christ-followers. Even if the corporate worship events did not manage to attain a perfect balance of music from the ages, the music ministry created memories that will linger for a long time to come.

Congress 2010 was a time to care. Participants prepared 30,000 meal packages for needy people, some of whom were the street people of

Honolulu. It was very encouraging to see the glad participation of Baptists of all ages combining their efforts in preparing meal packages for the materially poor.

Congress 2010 was not for adults alone. Special programs were prepared for the children and the youth. Organizers seized the opportunity to offer relevant experiences for the target groups and the response was very encouraging.

This report on the Baptist World Congress in Hawai`i is intended as an official record of the event. May it also remind us of the celebration that will mark our coming together in the presence of the risen Lord at the end of the age!

If we believe that the Spirit spoke to us in Honolulu, we must now begin anew the Christian journey in step with the Spirit as we implement the focus for the next five years in the life of the BWA.

Neville Callam
General Secretary
Baptist World Alliance

PART I
INTRODUCTION

1. Overview of the Congress

Eron Henry

There are several things that mark a Baptist World Congress such as the one held in Honolulu, Hawai`i, from July 28 to August 1, 2010. Words used to describe this once-every-five-year international event include "diversity," "empowering experience," "wonderful fellowship," "refreshing," "a gathering of a great cloud of witnesses," and "great memories."

Those who were privileged to be in Honolulu experienced all these and more. Several weeks after the Honolulu meetings, Regina Claas, general secretary for the German Baptist union and a BWA vice president wrote, "I have been waking up every morning with such joy in my heart and song in my soul, knowing that this congress has moved many people and will have far-reaching effects in the global Baptist family and beyond." Claas' counterpart in Britain, Jonathan Edwards, wrote, "The most striking thing about the congress is the diversity – diversity over everything apart from our common love of the Lord Jesus Christ."

There are those who were willing to make comparisons not only between the 2010 congress and past congresses, but also between this congress and all Baptist gatherings generally. "I have been to scores of large meetings and conventions," wrote Jim White, editor of the Virginia, USA, newspaper, *Religious Herald*, "but this one exceeded them all." "It was arguably the best Baptist meeting I have attended in recent years (and I attend a bunch of them)!" said Rob Nash, coordinator of global missions for the Cooperative Baptist Fellowship of the United States.

Great preaching, awesome music, warm fellowship

It appears that the meetings in Honolulu were particularly special because of the high level of preaching and the Bible studies. "Best preaching ever! Have been truly renewed and refreshed," a Facebook post stated. "Great speakers, and with contributions from all continents," David Kerrigan of BMS World Mission out of Britain noted. Another great benefit of a Baptist World Congress is that it enables Baptists from all over the world to hear outstanding preachers and Bible teachers that they would have had little opportunity to hear of, or from, otherwise. Though all the preachers and Bible teachers were well known among Baptists within their own countries and regions, the wider Baptist family now knows Alongla Aier, Janet Clark, Allan Demond, Paul Msiza, Karl Johnson, Pablo Deiros, and Lance Watson.

Others identified the International Music Fest held Thursday through Saturday as a highlight of their experience. These concert-type presentations featured performers from Canada, India, Latvia, Nigeria, Trinidad and Tobago, the United States, and elsewhere. Music arrangements included African contemporary blends, classical, choral and traditional music. "One of my favorite parts of the event was hearing the music represented from around the world. The International Music Fest each day was quite unique with various countries represented there as well," one blog posting read. The vast diversity in musical styles used in worship is exposed during a congress, and it was so in Honolulu. It was clearly shown that Baptists have included musical forms and styles from their own cultures into worship, demonstrating that western musical forms do not have a monopoly on the Baptist worship experience. Exposure to such a rich musical feast may encourage churches to be more open to including in their liturgies or orders of worship forms of music from their own and other cultures.

Baptists traveled thousands of miles, some over several days at great expense, to share in the great fellowship that comes with meeting Baptists from all over the world. Ninety-five year old Geoffrey Blackburn from Australia, is a former BWA vice president. He has attended twelve consecutive congresses, every congress since 1955, including the Hawai`i congress. He recalled his first experience of the 1955 congress in London.

"The first thing I noticed was the multinational nature of the delegates... There were the Norwegian, Finnish and Swedish women in their colorful national dresses and bonnets. Also delegates from many African and Asiatic countries." The opportunity to meet and have fellowship with such a vast and diverse group has impelled Blackburn to make the long and arduous journey to each congress. Faith Bowers of the United Kingdom said that "for me, the great joy of these occasions is sharing our common faith with people from different cultures." Tunrayo Adegbilero from Nigeria, president of the Baptist Women's Union of Africa, said of her first congress in Birmingham, England, in 2005, "I was awed by the attendance... I did not know Baptists existed in so many nations of the world." Luz-Maria Lopez of Chile said, "It's a good idea to merge different cultures, to be able to come together with the Lord, to share experience." Donald Kelly from Maryland in the United States endorsed the power of the fellowship shared at the congress. "The fellowship can develop by having these friends around the world and other people that go through the same struggle that you are going through."

A great feature of Baptist congresses, especially the congress in Hawai`i, is that the entire family can participate. There were activities for teens and younger children where they were able to meet with others of their own age group from a country and culture that may have be alien to their own. The congress was a wonderful time and place for young Baptists to come to the realization that there are other children of God and followers of Jesus Christ who are different from who they are – racially, ethnically, culturally. Yet these are also authentic followers of and believers in the Lord Jesus Christ.

Each Baptist World Congress is also an opportunity for networking as the congress is one of the international settings where Baptist groups can make connections on a one-on-one, face-to-face basis, forging partnerships and joint ministry ventures. In Honolulu, one would see small groups of persons from various countries huddled together in intense and earnest discussions between meetings and sessions. Seminary leaders, professors and lecturers were able to make important connections across countries and continents. Mission leaders and missioners were able to fellowship and share experiences and programs. The congress also created a space for Baptists from various regions to meet others from their own regions. Asia and Africa, for instance, are vast continents where opportunities for Baptists to meet each other may be few and far between. Baptists from West Africa, such as Liberia, can meet Baptists from East Africa, such as Tanzania. French-speaking Baptists from Togo and other countries can meet English-speaking Baptists from Kenya and elsewhere. East Asian Baptists from South Korea and Japan may have the opportunity to meet and share with Baptists from Southeast Asia, including Indonesia and the Philippines.

Indeed, the meetings in Hawai`i were a powerful demonstration of the ability of the BWA to bring Baptists together and to bring all Baptists into one fold. This was most clearly demonstrated through the presence of the general secretary of the Baptist Churches in Vietnam (BCV). The BCV received official membership into the BWA, along with the Baptist Fellowship of Zambia and the District of Columbia Baptist Convention from the United States, during the BWA General Council meeting which was held on the morning of July 28, 2010 prior to the formal start of the congress.

The presence of the BCV in Hawai`i did not happen by accident. In May 2006 a BWA delegation led by outgoing BWA President David Coffey made a human rights trip to Vietnam where it was discovered that there were at least five distinct Baptist groups, one of which was the BCV. That BWA visit paved the way and opened the door for the BCV to receive official government recognition, which occurred in October 2008. Formed formally in 1988, the BCV includes 509 churches and approximately 30,000 members, a testament to the strength of the church in the country, something that was largely unknown to Baptists around the world.

Baptists reaching beyond self

The congress enabled Baptists to stretch themselves in addressing matters of life and ministry. The focus groups, reported on in much greater detail in chapter thirteen, led Baptists to reflect on concerns that are problematic and challenging both within and outside the church. Christians and churches cannot ignore many of these issues over the long term as these issues become more and more pressing, demanding attention and action. Certainly Christians, including Baptists, who live in countries where theirs is a minority faith, cannot ignore the challenge of relating to persons of other faith traditions, one of the seventeen topics explored in the various focus groups. Nabil Costa of Lebanon, elected at the congress as a BWA vice president, said of Muslims, "If they are our enemies, Jesus said we are to love them. If they are our neighbors, Jesus said we are to love them. So either we love them as enemies or love them as neighbors, that's our only choice."

Congress participants were reminded of the need to engage in practical ministry by reaching out to others and helping to meet their needs. Approximately 300 participants were engaged in a meal packaging event at the congress where a total of 30,000 rice-based meals, consisting of dehydrated, high-protein and highly-nutritious food, were prepared. In addition to packaging meals, nearly 800 hygiene kits were packaged by congress participants and given to the Institute for Human Services (IHS), a local homeless shelter, for distribution. Other volunteers sorted clothing and other donated items at the IHS. Another group painted a hallway and stairwell at the homeless shelter.

The congress is also an opportunity to give recognition to those who have served well with one highlight being the BWA Quinquennial Human Rights Award. Previous recipients of this award include former United States President Jimmy Carter. The 2010 recipient was Denton Lotz, former general secretary of the BWA, who was recognized for a lifetime of commitment to human rights concerns. Lotz was described as an "outstanding Baptist leader," a "persistent human rights campaigner," a "courageous advocate," and a "visionary." While the aforementioned focus groups were not tailored to give recognition to persons, there were nevertheless, occasions for others to come into an awareness of the work being done by committed Baptists to confront, or experience, some of the greatest evils on the planet. Such evils include human trafficking and ethnic and religious persecution. Participants were able to hear from persons such as Zhanuo Sanchu and Lauran Bethell, the 2005 recipient of the Quinquennial Human Rights Award, who work with women and children that experience the worst forms of exploitation; and from Blooming Night Zan on the consequences of living under, and having to flee from, a repressive government regime. A press conference was held where Wati Aier, a leader in the Forum for Naga Reconciliation, spoke of the quest to end the decades-long conflict among the Naga people; and from Leena Lavanya, who, for more than 15 years, has engaged in various ministries to lift up the downtrodden in the South Indian state of Andhra Pradesh, including those who suffer from HIV/AIDS.

New leadership

It is at each congress that the leadership of the BWA is elected to serve for the next five-year term; it is the occasion for the passing of the guard. Coffey concluded his five years of service after taking the lead to make some profound changes to the BWA. Among Coffey's initiatives was the formation of the BWA Emerging Leaders Network, created to identify potential Baptist leaders who, over the past several years, met during the BWA Annual Gathering. Coffey was the driving force behind the formation of the Implementation Task Force which completed its work during the period and made recommended changes to the BWA, including changes to the size and makeup of the BWA Executive Committee and other constitutional reforms. It was also during Coffey's tenure that the BWA elected Neville Callam as BWA general secretary, succeeding Lotz who retired in 2007. Coffey stated that "It has been an inestimable privilege to serve as the BWA president. The opportunities for international ministry have been immense and the capacity for personal spiritual development has gone beyond all expectations. The prayers of those who have followed my global journeys have been a sustaining power for my ministry."

New president John Upton has held various posts in the organization before being elected president, including being chair of the Congress Program Committee that helped to plan the 2010 congress in Hawai`i. He served as a member of the BWA General Council and the Executive Committee, the two governing bodies of the BWA. He was a member of the Baptist World Aid Committee, the Commission on Christian Ethics, and the Executive Committee of the North American Baptist Fellowship, one of six regional fellowships of the BWA. He is part of a new team that includes Callam, who has day to day responsibility for the affairs of the BWA and who demonstrated his giftedness as a leader and administrator in leading the planning of the congress. Other leaders elected to serve for the 2010-2015 period include 12 vice presidents, two from each of the six regions of the BWA – Africa, Asia/Pacific, Caribbean, Europe, Latin America, and North America. The BWA welcomed a new regional secretary for the Caribbean, Everton Jackson. Both the men's and women's departments elected new executives, with Owen Crooks of Jamaica the new president for the BWA Men's Department, and Raquel Contreras from Chile the new president for the BWA Women's Department.

Ecumenical friends and partners

Even though the congress was a gathering of Baptists, the event nevertheless reminded Baptists that we are part of a larger Christian family with whom we share a common faith and commitment to Jesus Christ. Leaders from two of the largest ecumenical groups in the world, the World Council of Churches and the World Evangelical Alliance, brought greetings. Some 25 Baptist conventions and unions from various countries hold membership in the WCC, while the WEA includes a number of Baptist denominational bodies and parachurch organizations. Greetings were also received from the Vatican's Pontifical Council for Promoting Christian Unity. Both the BWA and the Pontifical Council have been engaged in theological conversations since 2006, following previous talks that were held from 1984 to 1988. The current talks end in 2010 after which an official report will be published.

Beginning in the 1980s, BWA leaders have visited the China Christian Council. The most recent delegation was led by Coffey in early 2010 to Beijing, Nanjing, Hangzhou, and Shanghai. Since 1985, leaders of the CCC have attended every Baptist World Congress. The CCC, which includes a number of churches that were originally Baptist, was founded in 1980 as an umbrella organization for all Protestant churches in the vast East Asian country. Present in Hawai`i were Xu Xiaohong, secretary general of the National Committee of the Three Self Patriotic Movement of the CCC, who brought greetings, and Wen Ge, a professor at the Nanjing Theological Seminary.

Other ecumenical partners and guests at the congress were representatives of the Mennonite World Conference, the General Conference of the Seventh-day Adventist Church, and the Lutheran World Federation.

Lasting legacy

The congress is not an end in itself. It serves as a springboard for the focus of the program for the next five years. The 2010 congress theme was "Hear the Spirit." Over the next five years, the theme that will guide the program for the BWA will be "In Step with the Spirit," the same theme that was used by the BWA Women's Department at its Women's Leadership Conference, which was one of the events that preceded the congress. Various subthemes related to the overarching theme will be explored and executed in the programs, activities and events planned by the BWA between 2010 and 2015.

Based on a report from the Hawai'i Tourism Authority, the city of Honolulu and the state of Hawai'i appeared to be happy to have so many Baptists visiting. President and CEO of the authority, Mike McCartney, stated, "The Baptist World Congress... helped boost the total number of visitors here for conventions, meetings and incentives with a 23.5 percent increase from a year ago." Baptists are convinced that the congress resulted in much more than a boost to the economy of the state. The Spirit of Christ, expressed in the love, warmth and generosity of spirit that prevailed among Baptists, was shared in many ways in Honolulu. This is a lasting legacy that is difficult to quantify. It is a legacy left behind by every Baptist world congress, beginning with the first in 1905 in London. The 20th Baptist World Congress in Honolulu, Hawai'i, in 2010, was no less.

2. Greetings

World Evangelical Alliance
Rev. Dr. Geoff Tunnicliffe

Sisters and Brothers, today, I bring you warm Christian greetings in the name of the Triune God from the World Evangelical Alliance and the 420 million Christians we serve. As you meet together here in Hawai`i for your 20th Congress, you do so at an important juncture in history. The challenges facing humanity are both complex and immense. Today the church has a crucial role in responding to the current global reality.

We are deeply grateful for the role that Baptists play in the World Evangelical Alliance and our National Evangelical Alliances. In almost every Alliance, Baptists are playing a key leadership role. The inter-connectedness of Baptists and other evangelicals is a demonstration of your commitment to demonstrating the unity in the Body of Christ.

I recognize that the Baptist World Alliance shares many of the same concerns as the World Evangelical Alliance. Your commitment to world evangelism, proclaiming God's grace, serving the poor, speaking out for religious liberty, and a passion for the transformative work of the Holy Spirit, strikes a deep chord in the heart of all evangelical Christians.

It is our prayer that as you hear the Spirit and respond to His direction the Lord will continue to bless, guide and empower you as you seek to live out the liberating message of the Gospel. May the name of Christ be uplifted and His grace be proclaimed in all the nations of the world for the Glory of God.

With best wishes
Reverend Dr. Geoff Tunnicliffe
Secretary General/CEO

World Council of Churches
Presented by Rev. Dr. Bernice Powell Jackson

"May the God who gives endurance and encouragement give you a spirit of unity among yourselves as you follow Christ Jesus" (Romans 15:5).

Dear Brothers and Sisters, grace and peace to you in the name of our Lord and Savior, Jesus Christ.

It is indeed a privilege to offer the 20th Congress of the Baptist World Alliance (BWA) greetings on behalf of the World Council of Churches (WCC). The WCC is a fellowship of 349 Orthodox, Anglican, Protestant and United churches in more than 120 countries, all seeking to make their unity in Christ visible so that the world might believe in God's amazing love for all creation. Many of the denominations gathered in Hawai`i are among the churches sharing fellowship in the WCC and we give thanks to God for their witness and leadership.

I am grateful that the Rev. Dr. Bernice Powell-Jackson, one of the eight presidents of the WCC, is with you to deliver these words of encouragement and to stand with you in prayer and deliberations through the week. The Rev. Dr. Powell-Jackson and I were recently together in Haiti, where we witnessed firsthand the endurance of the Baptist believers in following Christ and the encouragement of the Baptist churches in rebuilding the community.

The theme under which you are gathered in Honolulu is a charge to prayerfully listen for what the Spirit of God is saying to the world today. It is a call to hear anew the Gospel of our Lord Jesus Christ, to see with fresh eyes the mission to which God is leading us and to be renewed with a sense of unity and purpose as a family of churches.

The Baptist churches have a rich history of sharing the Gospel with conviction, building up the body of Christ and serving the people of God. The Baptist World Alliance, like the WCC, grows out of the 19th century missionary movement marked by events such as the inaugural Baptist Congress in 1905 and the Edinburgh Missionary Conference of 1910. And much like the WCC, the BWA exists as an expression of the "oneness of Baptist people in the Lord Jesus Christ ... for sharing concerns and skills in witness and ministry."

This ecumenical missionary spirit that spoke to the churches more than 100 years ago was inspired by Jesus' prayer that his followers would be one, as Christ is one with the Father, so that world might believe (John 17:21). The unity for which Christ prayed is a gift from God, given by grace through the life, death and resurrection of our Lord and Savior. As Paul reminds the Romans, God grants endurance and encouragement, but also a spirit of unity among Christ's followers so that the Gospel will be known throughout the world.

The call for Christian unity and common witness is as urgent today as it was 2,000 years ago; and as it was 100 years ago. The divine invitation to be united in Christ for the sake of God's mission in the world is a prayer we are called to answer. The WCC looks to the Baptist World Alliance with the hope of growing in partnership for this purpose. Baptist churches play a key role in global Christianity, being both ecumenical and evangelical in spirit and witness. As we discover new relationships in the service of Christian unity, we look to Baptist churches for guidance and wisdom, prayer and leadership.

In the days ahead, as you listen for the Spirit, as you pray together, as you testify to one another and as you discuss the future of the Baptist World Alliance, it is the earnest prayer of the World Council of Churches that God may bless this congress with a spirit of unity, that Christ may inspire this congress in witnessing to the love of God and that the Holy Spirit may be heard through the songs, prayers and statements of this congress.

Rev. Dr. Olav Fykse Tveit
General Secretary

Pontifical Council for Promoting Christian Unity
Presented by Rev. Dr. Gregory J. Fairbanks

Brothers and sisters in the Lord, "grace and peace to you from God our Father and the Lord Jesus Christ" (1 Cor 1:3).

On behalf of Archbishop Kurt Koch, president of the Pontifical Council for Promoting Christian Unity, the Vatican Department for Ecumenism, I bring you prayerful greetings on behalf of the Catholic Church.

It is a great honor for me to attend this 20th Baptist World Congress devoted to "Hearing the Spirit" as an ecumenical guest. Allow me to say that the current phase of theological conversations between the Catholic Church and the Baptist World Alliance, which began in 2006, is being conducted in that same attitude of Hearing the Spirit. The theme of the conversations are "The Word of God in the Life of the Church: Scripture, Tradition and Koinonia." As Pope Benedict XVI expressed to the participants in the conversations, "If our hope for reconciliation and greater fellowship between Baptists and Catholics is to be realized, issues such as these need to be faced together, in a spirit of openness, mutual respect and fidelity to the liberating truth and saving power of the Gospel of Jesus Christ. As believers in Christ, we acknowledge him as the one mediator between God and humanity (1 Timothy 2:5), our Savior, our Redeemer. He is the cornerstone (Ephesians 2:21; 1 Peter 2:4-8); and the head of the body, which is the church" (Col 1:18).

It is in this same spirit of openness, mutual respect and fidelity to the liberating truth and saving power of the Gospel of Jesus Christ that I extend the prayerful best wishes of the Catholic Church to this Baptist World Congress. It is my prayer that these days will be a time to Hear the Spirit alive in our hearts, because the world needs our common witness to Christ and to the hope brought by the Gospel.

Mennonite World Conference
Presented by Rev. David Wiebe

President David Coffey, General Secretary Neville Callam and dear sisters and brothers in the Lord: I bring you greetings on behalf of the Mennonite World Conference (MWC) and General Secretary Larry Miller and President Danisa Ndlovu.

Thank you, Brother Neville Callam, for the invitation to attend your event and the warm, generous hospitality extended to me.

The roots of the Mennonites are found in the Anabaptist reformation of the 1500s in central Europe. Menno Simons of Holland was a significant leader and from him comes our name.

We have strong connections to the Baptists. During the 1700s Mennonites moved into southern Russia and developed a significant presence there. During the communist regime of the 20th century there were really only two options for church identity – Orthodox and Baptist. We weren't Orthodox, so Mennonites became Baptists in Russia. It seems that some folks in your fellowship have a "Mennonite alter ego." It's also significant that Mennonites and Baptists have conversed to work through aspects of difference and similarity as larger movements.

Most recently a Lutheran-Mennonite International Study Commission worked from 2005-2009 to address the fact that the Augsburg Confession contains several anathemas against Anabaptists. A report entitled "Healing of Memories: Reconciling in Christ" has been tabled at the Lutheran World Federation Congress this past week.

Last Thursday, Dr. Ishmael Noko, the LWF General Secretary led a special service, calling worshippers to "remember how Anabaptist Christians knew suffering and persecution, and how some of the most honored Reformation leaders defended this persecution in the name of faithfulness."

Bishop Danisa Ndlovu, MWC president, responded to say, "Today, in this place, we together – Lutherans and Anabaptist Mennonites – are fulfilling the rule of Christ." Dr. Larry Miller, General Secretary of MWC, confessed that Anabaptist-Mennonite communities are also "in need of healing and forgiveness."

Following prayers of confession, the service moved into "envisioning the future together" and sowing the seeds of reconciliation and peace.

Sisters and brothers, God is at work building his church! Some issues take 500 years to solve. Let us persevere in "looking unto Jesus, the author and finisher of our faith" and let us hear the Spirit as He directs us into unity as a church for the mission of His Kingdom.

God bless you. Mahalo.

Seventh-day Adventist Church
Dr. John Graz

Aloha!

Dear Brothers and sisters, on behalf of the General Conference of the Seventh-day Adventist and nearly 30 million people in the worldwide Adventist family living in 205 countries around the world, I am very pleased and honored to bring you greetings from your brothers and sisters in Jesus.

We believe Adventists and Baptists have many things in common. William Miller, one of our founding fathers, was a Baptist preacher. From the Seventh-day Baptists we receive the Saturday Sabbath. We share with you the same love for the Bible as God's Word; the same practice of baptism by immersion; the same fact about Jesus' commission to preach the gospel to every nation and people; and we share the common hope in his soon return.

We receive from you our love for religious freedom and in many parts of the world we are united to defend and promote it. Often, where you are persecuted we are persecuted too. When those of us are persecuted human rights and freedom are denied.

On behalf of my church I want to say a special thanks to your General Secretary, Dr. Neville Callam, who is a great ambassador of the Baptist family around the world and who has become a friend. I would like to also thank your former General Secretary, Dr. Denton Lotz, for his friendship, his outstanding Christian testimony and his commitment to religious freedom.

Thank you very much for inviting me and may God bless the 20th Congress of the Baptist World Alliance.

Dr. John Graz
Director, Department of Public Affairs and Religious Liberty
The General Conference of the Seventh-day Adventist Church

Lutheran World Federation
Presented by Bishop Murray Finck

Aloha, sisters and brothers in Christ.

The grace, promise and joy of our living Lord Jesus be with you all and bless your congress here in Honolulu.

Thank you for the honor and the privilege of being with you. Your warmth and hospitality has been a gift as I come on behalf of the Lutheran World Federation which is headquartered in Geneva, Switzerland. The Lutheran World Federation, which we call LWF, is made up of 140 Lutheran churches in seventy-nine different countries. It encompasses roughly seventy million Lutheran Christians around the world.

With you we are hearing and listening to the Holy Spirit of God. With you we are centered in our faith and life in Christ Jesus and in his abundant grace. With you we believe the Spirit of God moves among us, calls us to faith, gifts us, inspires and leads us as children of God. With you we believe in and we pray for the grace of our Lord Jesus Christ, the love of God and the communion of the Holy Spirit to be with us all. Although we differ in our faith traditions, as brothers and sisters in Christ we have more in common than that which separates us.

I bring you greetings on behalf of the president of the Lutheran World Federation, the Reverend Mark Hanson, and the general secretary of LWF, Dr. Ishmael Noko. Just last week the Lutheran World Federation was meeting and I thank a previous speaker for telling the story that brings healing to the Lutheran and Anabaptist community. In that same meeting the Reverend Munib Younan from Jerusalem was elected as the new president and the Reverend Martin Junge as general secretary. I bring greetings on their behalf too.

According to the seventeenth chapter of the Gospel of John, Jesus prayed for unity among his followers. Most of the Lutheran faith communities believe that dialogue and intentional conversation with all sisters and brothers in Christ is necessary for us as followers of Jesus. Our lives and our faith is richer and fuller and our witness is more authentic when we are committed to be in the same room with each other in dialogue with one another; when our voices and our hands and our feet work together in ministry that strives for peace and justice; when we share in efforts to care for each other, especially for those who are in need, those in peril, those in want, those in pain and when we all together are called to be stewards of God's good creation. The more we discover the ways that Jesus' prayer for unity can become our reality, the greater our Christian witness will be in a world so in need of the living Lord.

The Apostle Paul states that there is one body, one Spirit, one Lord, one faith, one baptism, one God and Father of us all. We believe this is our challenge together to discover more and more ways as the body of Christ to live in that oneness. We truly need one another to be the fullest expression of the Body of Christ. Thank you for giving witness to that in this gathering.

A final thought. I am one of 65 Bishops of the Evangelical Lutheran Church in America and I serve the most southern part of California and Hawai`i and it is never a disappointment for me to be called to the work here in Hawai`i. I see a missionary spirit here among the people and churches on these islands. I see a missionary spirit among the leaders in this diverse mixture of humanity in this most remote place on earth. On the Big Island I see the Spirit of God continuing to hover over that island as God continues the work of creation building and fashioning that island day by day as the lava flows from the core of the earth. There is a spirit here that the Hawaiian people call Aloha and it is filled with warmth and reception. You have come to a good place to hear the Spirit. Thank you for inviting me and those that I represent to be with you as we listen to the breath of God.

China Christian Council
Presented by Rev. Xu Xiaohong

Dear Dr. Coffey; dear Dr. Neville Callam, general secretary of the BWA; dear distinguished guests, dear colleagues, dear brothers and sisters:

First of all, I bring you warmest greetings from the Chinese churches in Christ! Aloha!

It is such a great honor for me and my colleague Rev. Wen Ge, representing the China Christian Council and the National Committee of the Three-Self Patriotic Movement, to be invited to witness this great event. Meanwhile, we are also very delighted to meet our Chinese Baptist brothers and sisters from Hong Kong and Taiwan.

CCC and the National TSPM have a very friendly relationship with the BWA. This January, a BWA delegation led by Rev. David Coffey visited the Chinese churches. We had a wonderful sharing and exchange together on our mutual concerns about church development.

As you may know, two miracles are happening in China. One is the economic development out of China's 30-year reform and openness to the world, and the other is the dramatic growth of Chinese churches. According to 2009 statistics, there are more than 20 million protestant Christians in China with more than 60,000 churches and meeting points. From 1980 to the end of last year, more than 51.17 million copies of the Bible have been printed and published in China. Besides, we have also published more than 300 kinds of devotional literature with more than 40 million copies. Now there are 20 seminaries and Bible colleges in China that have trained more than 10,000 seminarians for ministry.

The great development of the Chinese churches results from "hearing the Spirit." It is more important that, through self-support, self-administration and self-propagation, the Chinese churches have explored a unique way for church growth that fits the Chinese churches well. There are no longer denominations in China. According to the scriptural teaching, the Chinese churches are in a postdenominational stage, continuing to unite in Christ.

So far in China there have not appeared such great evangelists as St. Peter, who was filled by the Spirit and successfully converted 3,000 or 5,000 people through only one remarkable preaching. The characteristic way that the Chinese churches do mission is through each individual Chinese Christian.

As you may know, there are not enough pastors in China. But so far we have more than 190,000 church lay workers to take their place. The Chinese churches underscore mission and evangelism. The Chinese Christians, however, are doing mission by following the Apostle Philip who keeps inviting Chinese Nathaniels to "come and see." The senior pastor whom I used to work with always says that a pastor is mainly responsible for organizing God's people. He points out that it is not the shepherd, but the sheep that can bear sheep. In the same vein, only life can bring about life. This leads to the great miracle of the rapid growth of the Chinese churches.

Finally, on behalf of CCC and the National TSPM, I wish this congress a great success with the Spirit's guidance. My hope is that the Chinese churches and the BWA, on the basis of mutual respect, can work together and strive together for the furtherance of the Gospel. May the friendship and fellowship between the Chinese churches and the BWA shine as the warm sunshine of Hawai`i.

Thank you very much!

John Upton
President, Baptist World Alliance

3. The Congress Message

The Baptist World Alliance is a global movement of Baptists sharing a common confession of faith in Jesus Christ bonded together by God's love to support, encourage and strengthen one another while proclaiming and living the gospel of Jesus Christ in the power of the Holy Spirit before a lost and hurting world.

At the 20th Baptist World Congress, meeting July 28-August 1, 2010, in Honolulu, Hawai`i:

We came
- to hear what the Spirit is saying to the church
- to experience the fellowship of the global Baptist family
- to feel the security of being embraced by brothers and sisters from around the globe

We heard
- the "Aloha" of the Hawaiian people and experienced their spirit of hospitality
- the vital importance of living and leading in the anointing of the Holy Spirit
- that we must reclaim the urgency of proclaiming a liberating gospel that brings about transformation
- the testimonies of brothers and sisters who have experienced persecution, oppression, marginalization, natural disasters and human-induced disaster
- the challenge to share the power of the gospel of Christ to rescue those living without the hope of Christ

We saw
- the beauty of God's good creation
- diversity in cultural expression, dress and worship styles
- the unity of the global family and the joy of friendship in Christ

Now, in step with the Spirit who gives and redeems life in Jesus Christ, we confess anew that all persons are created in the image of God and are therefore worthy of receiving his redemptive grace.

In step with the Spirit, we renew our commitment to:

- communicate, in the power of the Holy Spirit, the truth of God in Jesus Christ as the hope of the world. Because the Spirit of the Lord is upon us, we have been anointed to:
  - develop greater familiarity with the teachings of Christ
  - cultivate a rich prayer life
  - bear witness to the Gospel of salvation through Jesus Christ
  - provide examples of godly living reflecting the values taught by the Lord of the church

- support the values reflected in the UN Millennium Development Goals. Because the Spirit of the Lord is upon us, we have been anointed us to:
  - remove the scourge of poverty and hunger
  - support efforts to provide universal education
  - work for environmental sustainability
  - promote gender equality
  - improve child health and maternal health
  - combat HIV/AIDS, malaria and other diseases
  - develop global partnerships

Enabled by the Spirit, let us commit ourselves to create an environment in which God's mercy and truth become evident. Let us shine the light of God's love in every place of human need.

PART II

SERMONS & BIBLE STUDIES AT PLENARY SESSIONS

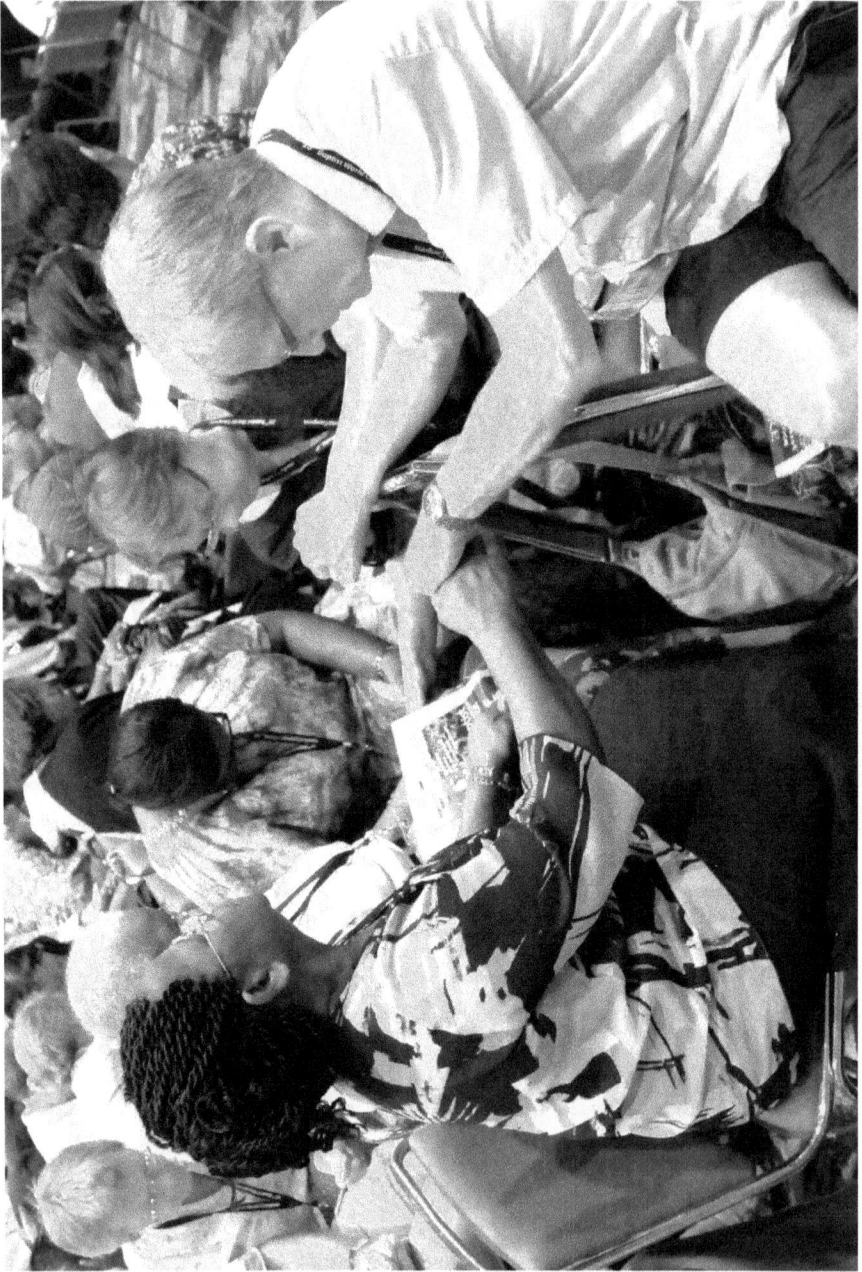

4. Consecration (Sermon)

David Coffey

"The Spirit of the Lord is on me because he has anointed me..." (Luke 4:18a).

When my friends discovered I was flying to Hawai`i for the BWA Congress they reacted in a variety of ways. Some friends were envious and said, "I wish I was coming with you;" others were curious and asked, "Why have you chosen the exotic venue, Hawai`i?" to which I replied, "Why not Hawai`i!" Some of my friends were full of good wishes and said they would be praying we would have a spiritually rich congress. And some added the personal comment that they considered it was most romantic for my wife Janet and me to be in the paradise setting of Hawai`i!

My surname is "Coffey," which originates from Ireland and all four of my grandparents were Irish born and bred. You may be aware that the Irish are renowned as incurable romantics and not surprisingly I have inherited this in my personality. A few months ago I was at Victoria Station in London waiting for a train. It was early morning and over the loudspeakers I heard the music of one of my wife's favorite songs, so feeling romantic I thought I would send her a text. The text read, "I am listening to your favorite song and thinking of you – I love you very much – David." And then in an act of romantic madness I added two kisses to the text.

My romantic heart expected an instant reply from my wife but there was no response. No text, not even a tweet, and I felt very downcast and rejected. I carried on my work through the day and completed my lectures at Spurgeon's College and late afternoon I was on the train making my way home to Oxfordshire when I received a text. But it was not from my wife, Janet – it was from a friend of mine called Steve. His message read: "Was this text intended for me?" My message with the two kisses had gone to him! A message intended for Janet's eyes only had gone astray.

Now here is the point. Every time we open God's Word there is a message for our eyes only. As Baptists we believe that God speaks through his living Word and every day of this BWA congress there will be a message for our eyes only. As we come to the living Word, let us approach it as lively people expecting that God has a word for us. Don't let God's message go astray!

Our congress theme is "Hear the Spirit," and this theme is unquestionably a deep challenge to all our lives and ministries; but as we lead our churches and manage our Christian organizations the leading question is, which spirit is guiding our thinking? Is it the self-dependent spirit that imagines the harder you work, the more you achieve? This worldly spirit of pure activism can invade the life of the church and lead us to believe that so long as we are busy with our programs and strategies we are guaranteed spiritual blessing. Specific strategies and managed programs do have the potential to enrich our mission and bless a needy world, but I urge you to heed this warning about the true source of our spiritual energy and vision. You can be a purpose driven church; a seeker sensitive church; an emergent and creative church; a justice and peace church; a conservative Calvinist church - but whatever the tradition of our church, if we fail to hear the Holy Spirit of the Living God, then all our serving will be futile and fruitless.

I urge you to never embark on your ministry without listening to the Spirit! It is possible to have the appointing without the anointing. You can have all the appointments, but none of the anointments; you can have all the titles, but none of the authority; you can have all the programs, but none of the power. Seek the anointing of the Holy Spirit on your life and ministry! This was the way of Jesus. He was the one who commenced his mission ministry in the pulpit at Nazareth with the words, "The Spirit of the Lord is upon me because he has anointed me" (Luke 4:18b).

Luke clearly states that through the whole of his life Jesus operates in the realm of the Spirit. The Holy Spirit is integral to his virgin birth because Jesus was conceived by the Holy Spirit and born of the Virgin Mary (Luke

1:34-35). At his baptism, the divine identity of Jesus is affirmed by an action of the Holy Spirit. The heaven was opened and the Holy Spirit descended upon Jesus in bodily form like a dove, and the voice came from heaven: "You are my beloved Son and with you I am well pleased" (Luke 3:21-22).

Then, full of the Holy Spirit, Jesus is led by the Spirit into the wilderness of temptation where for 40 days he was tempted by the devil (Luke 4:1-13). This is the testing of Jesus' consecration to God. Will he serve God's way and will he trust God to provide for his needs? Jesus battles with the lure of lies that could lead him away from the path of servant leadership, but, in the power of the Spirit, Jesus defeats Satan and emerges victorious from the wilderness of temptations. It's as if Jesus draws a line in the sand of the desert and proclaims: "I will serve God's way or not at all." Then Jesus, filled with the Holy Spirit, commences his teaching and healing ministry and one day he stands in the Nazareth pulpit and declares boldly, "The Spirit of the Lord is upon me" (Luke 4:16-30)!

Friends, can you see from the plain teaching of the Gospel record that the Spirit of the Lord is upon Jesus for his earthly origins, his messianic identity and his power to preach and heal? So why is it that so often in our ministries we choose to go it alone? This congress theme of "Hear the Spirit" could be a most significant moment in the history of our movement because so often as Baptists we are deaf to the Spirit. We choose our way and our methods and our timing and when we behave like this I suggest we are not walking in the footsteps of those Baptists who have gone before. John Smyth and Thomas Helwys heard the Spirit; it was because Lottie Moon and Martin Luther King heard the Spirit in their lifetime that they accomplished great things for Jesus.

God's purpose is that the Spirit-filled ministry of Jesus should continue today through all his people. Jesus promised the gift of his Holy Spirit in his farewell words: "You will have power to be my witnesses when the Holy Spirit comes" (Acts 1:8). On the day of Pentecost, Jesus fulfilled his promise and sent us the gift of His Spirit and now the Lord of the church expects all his people to say, "The Spirit of the Lord is on me, I am an anointed person."

The essence of the Holy Spirit's ministry is to bring the presence of Christ to his people. His purpose is that the Lord Jesus Christ is loved, honored, and praised (John 16:14). The desire of the Holy Spirit is to see Jesus preeminent in his church. Jim Packer suggests it's as if the Holy Spirit stands behind us throwing light over our shoulder so that the light shines on Jesus who is facing us. The message of the Holy Spirit is never, "Look at me, listen to me, get to know me." The role of the Holy Spirit is always: "Look at Jesus and see his glory; listen to Jesus and hear his word; go to Jesus and receive his life." In a memorable image, Packer suggests the Holy Spirit is the matchmaker, the celestial marriage broker, who brings us and Christ together and ensures we stay together.[1]

We have arrived in the beautiful land of Hawai`i ready to enjoy some new experiences this week. Mark Twain once described Hawai`i as "one long delicious summer day," and coming from rain-soaked England, I am looking forward to this experience! Another experience we have already encountered is the unique Aloha spirit of Hawai`i; truly the warmth and hospitality of the Hawaiian people is a wonderful experience. With invitations to the Polynesian Cultural Center and the historic Pearl Harbor we are guaranteed many new experiences this congress week, but there are two key spiritual experiences you need to be sure about if you want God's best from this congress.

You need to testify first that "The Holy Spirit is in me," and second, that the "The Holy Spirit is on me." For if you can't say the Holy Spirit is in me then you cannot be truly part of God's family and if you can't say the Holy Spirit is on me you will never be effective in ministry. If you say to me this evening, David, how can I experience these truths personally? Then my answer would be to ask if you have been born again of the Spirit by faith in Jesus? Have you received by God's grace the gift of new life? Are you able to say: "I have been crucified with Christ and I no longer live but Christ lives in me and the life I now live, I live by faith in the Son of God who loved me and died for me" (Galatians 2:20)?

---

[1] J.I. Packer, *Keep in Step with the Spirit,* Leicester, England: IVP, 1984, p.66.

When the Holy Spirit is in you then the love of God is poured into your heart (Romans 5:5). Some of you can testify this evening to the inner courage the Holy Spirit gives us. When you were standing in a courtroom on trial for being a follower of Jesus, the Holy Spirit made you a bold witness and taught you "at the very hour" what to say (Luke 12:12). Many of you here have experienced the comforting peace of the Holy Spirit during the great storms of life (John 14:16). We have stood in solidarity this year with those who suffered because of the devastating storms of sorrow and destruction that suddenly came upon the nations of Haiti and Chile. When your little ship has been tossed about on the great oceans of life and you have limped into a safe harbor with your broken mast and torn sails and missing rudder, what testimony have you been able to declare to a watching world? Those who know the inner peace of the Holy Spirit the Comforter are the ones who can testify: "When I passed through the waters I did not drown" (Isaiah 43:2) and at the height of the storm Jesus was with me.

But if we know the Holy Spirit is in us, how can we be sure the Holy Spirit is on us? When the Holy Spirit is on us it shows because those who hear the Spirit follow the directions of Jesus, they are serious about obeying his words. This was the pattern of Jesus' life. He could only do what he saw the Father doing (John 5:19).

I am not sure a father and his son understood this spiritual principle of imitation. The father was going away from home on a business trip and said to his nine-year-old son, "I want you to help around the house while I am away and I want you to do what I normally do." The father had in mind clearing the dinner table; washing the dishes; putting out the trash. After a few days he returned from his business trip and asked his wife, "How did our son do while I was away?"

His wife replied, "Well, it was very strange. After breakfast he made himself a cup of coffee and went into the living room and sat down. He put on some loud music and read the newspaper for half an hour!" Be sure you are modeling your life on a worthy example.

Jesus said, "The Son can do nothing by himself; he can only do what he sees his Father doing because whatever the Father does the Son does also" (John 5:19). This is the pattern of life in the Spirit. When we listen to the Holy Spirit we can live in perfect harmony with the Holy Trinity. To paraphrase the words of Jesus, "You cannot do anything by yourselves, you can only do what you see me doing."

When the Holy Spirit is on us and Jesus is leading his people it shows! The Acts of the Apostles is an inspiring account of what happens when people listen to the Spirit and follow Jesus on mission. In page after page of Acts we see that when the Holy Spirit is on people it produces healthy churches and fruitful mission; the Holy Spirit inspires praise and worship; he creates fellowship between diverse people; he gives wisdom and discernment; he exposes dishonesty in the church; he guides people in choosing church leaders; he drives the church into the adventures of evangelism; he brings us to new mission frontiers and encourages us to cross boundaries. But the greatest sign of the "Holy Spirit on us" is when we discover that God has included us in his action plan for winning a lost world. It's an eye popping moment when we realize our calling is not to be passive spectators but gifted actors in the unfolding drama of salvation's story.

You are probably aware that Hawai`i is a major center for the film industry and about twenty minutes drive from this Congress Hall is the film set for the cult TV series, "Lost," in June 2010, Walt Disney productions began making "On Stranger Tides", the latest movie in the "Pirates of the Caribbean" series; the long running television series "Hawaii Five-O" was filmed in this city, and the 2010 remake series will soon be released with a subtle change in the title. It's a zero rather than a capital "O"!

Now I confess I enjoy the occasional visit to the movies and like you I have sat in a darkened theater with my popcorn and drink. This is fine for when we are relaxing, but it is an unsuitable culture for mission ministry because the Holy Spirit is not interested in a spectator "popcorn and Coke" culture. We are not meant to sit back as if in a darkened movie theater watching a needy world flicker before our eyes. God does not intend us to be passive spectators; he has called and equipped us to be the actors in his great drama and has a part for each of us in his unfolding story of salvation. There is no application form to fill in; there is no audition to attend; all it requires is for every child of God to wake up and realize, "The Spirit of the Lord is on me and he has anointed me for service in his world." This gift is not just for preachers and pastors and missionaries; it is a promise for all followers of Jesus Christ.

I love the way Martin Luther King illustrated the power of the anointing. He would say: "If God calls you to be a street sweeper then sweep streets like Michelangelo painted pictures; sweep streets like Beethoven composed music; sweep streets like Shakespeare wrote poetry; sweep streets so well that all the hosts of heaven will have to pause and say 'Here lived a great street sweeper who did his job well!'"

When the Holy Spirit is on us the anointing shows! And this anointing enables us to face the most challenging of tasks.

Jesus chooses the Old Testament passage of Isaiah 61 as the starting point for his sermon in Nazareth where Isaiah describes scenes of utter devastation. There are ruined buildings and desolate communities; run down cities filled with broken-hearted people wearing sackcloth and ashes; places of devastation where people feel they are trapped in a prison of hopelessness; people burdened by poverty and spiritual blindness and crying out for a new beginning.

Isaiah faced an inherited brokenness with communities that had been "devastated for generations" (Isaiah 61:4). Do you realize the implications of this inherited brokenness? It means you could be facing a roadblock in your ministry caused by a previous generation. The cause of the roadblock happened long before you arrived on the scene but the impact of the inherited brokenness means people feel they are ruined forever. Their disposition is that nothing can change their situation because there has been "devastation for generations" and this creates a climate of extreme hopelessness.

Jesus faced this the day he came to Nazareth. He looked out on a congregation that represented the inherited brokenness of the villages and cities of his day. The families of poor farmers who were burdened because of harsh taxation systems (Luke 19:8); people whose lives had been destroyed by shame and guilt (Luke 7:36-50); the helplessness of people who had spent all their money on doctors and still were not cured (Luke 8:43); a community attempting to cope with the man who was called "the hopeless case" in the town. The community did not know how to cope with his demon possession so they wrapped him in chains and kept him under guard in the town cemetery (Luke 8:26-39). This is the despair of inherited brokenness.

Here we are in paradise for a few days but soon we will return home where daily we face the corrosive blight of inherited brokenness. We have left behind scenes of utter devastation with ruined buildings and desolate communities. Many of us work in run-down cities filled with broken-hearted people. We minister to people who feel they are trapped in prisons of hopelessness and perhaps we have come to this congress crying to the Lord for a new beginning for our mission ministry. Your heart cry is "Lord give me a breakthrough with this inherited brokenness that has held back our church through generations of devastation."

Well, I have good news for you! When the person anointed with the Holy Spirit speaks, the lives of people are transformed. The broken-hearted are healed; the bound are delivered; the prisoners are released (Isaiah 61:1). When the Spirit of the Lord is on us even bricks and mortar can be changed! The unfolding of the year of the Lord's favor means that ancient ruins are rebuilt; waste places are restored; ruined cities are renewed (Isaiah 61:4). The joyful message of Jubilee rolls back the years of devastation.

Surely all of us want to see the healing of this inherited brokenness in our communities because we are the followers of Jesus Christ who believe his church is called and created to make a difference in his world. We are the sent ones who have the words of Jesus burned into our lives: "As the Father has sent me so send I you" (John 20:21). We know that Jesus breathed on his disciples and said, "Receive the Holy Spirit," and therefore our prayer this evening should be, "Lord Jesus breathe on us, for when we have the anointing of the Spirit, our world can be changed."

Jesus said he shared his authority with his disciples (Luke 10:19), so why is it we stumble around the world as if we are a little people? We behave as if we are nobodies, but God says we are a chosen people! We say we have no status, but God says we are a royal priesthood! We declare we are unimportant, but God has granted us the title of a holy nation (1 Peter 2:9), and surely when the Spirit of the Lord is on us we should be deeply aware that we are the children of the King! These privileges indicate we are never a little people in God's eyes.

Many years ago in England there was a large shopping mall and adjacent to the mall was a tiny church, a little tin tabernacle building. One day the owners of the shopping mall wrote a letter to the leaders of the little tin tabernacle and said, we are thinking of expanding our business on this site and we need more land to build bigger premises. We would like to buy your tin tabernacle, so name your price.

The leaders of the church read the letter and after a few days they sent their reply. The letter said, "Thank you for sharing your plans for growth and expansion but as it happens we are thinking of expanding as we too would like to grow and develop. In fact we would like to buy your property and we invite you to name your price."

The members of the little tin tabernacle church were not fooling with the owners of the shopping mall because they had the resources to buy the shopping mall. The signature at the foot of the letter said it all. The letter had been signed by Mr. Cadbury who was the wealthy chocolate manufacturer and also a committed Christian. With his wealth he could have purchased every shopping mall in the country. Friends, the people of God are never a little people! The world may despise and hate us; the world may persecute us and seek to destroy us; the world may exercise a might without morality and a power without compassion. But the truth is, when the world has left the battlefield, the last people standing will be those who can exclaim, "The Spirit of the Lord is on me because he has anointed me."

God can give you a fresh anointing of His Holy Spirit to enable you to speak with power and serve with authority. You can experience the appointing and the anointing. You can enjoy the program and the power. You can carry all the titles with spiritual authority. The Lord desires you to finish the work he has given you to do.

Leonardo da Vinci was about to complete a painting he had been working on for months. Whilst working on the canvas he had been surrounded by a group of students who had been watching the master craftsman at work. As he reached the final stages of completing the painting, he handed the artist's brush to one of his students and said, "Finish it."

The student was astonished and stuttered the words, "But I have not got the talent. I am not worthy to finish it."

To which da Vinci responded, "Does not what I have done for you inspire you to do your best for me?"

Jesus says to us this evening, "Finish the ministry I have given you to do."

"Does not all I have done for you inspire you to do your best for me?"

And our response must be to offer our prayer of consecration at the beginning of this congress:

"Breathe on me breath of God
Fill me with life anew
That I may love what thou doest love
And do what thou wouldst do."
– Edwin Hatch

5. Proclamation (Bible Study)

Mr. President and Mr. General Secretary, thank you for this opportunity to address my Baptist brothers and sisters from all over the world.

Our Bible study deals with our commitment as we hear the Spirit, to proclaim the good news of the kingdom of God.

Our Scripture is in Luke 4:18 that in the New International Version (NIV) reads: "The Spirit of the Lord is on me because he has anointed me to preach good news ... he has sent me to proclaim freedom."

Introduction

I began to preach when I was fifteen years of age. My pastor, a well known Argentine evangelist, took me to an open-air meeting on a corner close to our Baptist church in the city of Rosario, Argentina. He gave me a microphone and told me: "Preach!" Two years later I began my studies at the International Baptist Theological Seminary in Buenos Aires, where now I serve as president. In the first few months I took a class of Theological English (most of our textbooks were in English in those years!) with a sweet Armenian-American lady. Almost every day she admonished us saying: "Preach the Word! We need Bible preachers!"

Through the last fifty years I've been trying to follow these admonitions and fulfill the call that I received from the Lord to preach and teach the Word. It has been my joy to serve Christ and His church through the proclamation of the Gospel. As a church historian I found this to be the very essence of the mission of a lively community of believers.

However, as an observer of the reality of the Christian mission around the world, I perceive in some places a notable decline in preaching. Sometimes it is due to the oblivion of the proclamation of the message of the Bible. Sometimes it is the result of announcing any "saving" message other than the Gospel. As Baptists we need to realize that the proclamation of the good news is the central task of the church. There is no church without this proclamation, and there is no other mission for the church than to proclaim Jesus as Lord in the power of the Holy Spirit.

As we consider our text, we see two imperatives related to the sharing of the Christian message: to preach and to proclaim. My prayer is that, as we pay attention to these two actions, we hear what the Spirit is saying to his church these days.

We should be preachers of good news

Our text says that the Messiah was sent "to preach good news." The Greek verb used here is *euaggelisasthai*. This expression was used in ancient Greek with regard to a slave who was announcing the victory of a general. The verb is used fifty-two times in the New Testament, twenty-five times by Luke and twenty-one by Paul. It simply means to announce or proclaim or to bring good news. Jesus describes his mission here as a preaching mission. His preaching of good news was directly connected with a demonstration of that good news. He had been sent to this world by his Father not merely to conduct preaching crusades, but to demonstrate the reality of the living God who is powerful enough to satisfy the personal needs of people. In fact, this was his answer to the inquiring disciples of John the Baptist. He did not preach an argumentative sermon but preached with redemptive actions that proved that "the good news was preached to the poor" (Luke 7:19-22).

In 2 Corinthians 5:20, Paul presents his foundation of authority as a Christian preacher when he says, "We implore you on Christ's behalf: Be reconciled to God." The Christian preacher is essentially God's herald. Preaching good news is the most sublime of all ministries. It was the highest priority of the Apostles, as it was in our Lord's own ministry. Mark 1:14 says that "Jesus went into Galilee, proclaiming the good news of God." The proclamation of the message of reconciliation should be the fundamental task in the ministry of every Christian who wants to serve with integrity. We are all called to be "preachers of good news." We become such when we take into account three factors.

Authority in Preaching

First, consider the importance of preaching. In the New Testament, the group of words related with preaching is among the most significant from a theological point of view. The concept of preaching is at the very heart of the apostolic faith and runs through almost every page in the New Testament. Paul was proud of considering himself as a "herald and apostle" and as he testifies in 1 Timothy 2:7, he was also appointed a "teacher of the true faith to the Gentiles." Besides, throughout the history of the Christian testimony, preaching has played a foundational role in the work of the church. The preaching and teaching of the good news related to Christ continues to be the number one responsibility of a committed Christian and a missional church.

We are truly a missional church when we understand that the church becomes a mission in following the Lord as an apostolic community that is in constant, dynamic movement, preaching the Gospel of the kingdom of light in the midst of the kingdom of darkness. There is no other church than the church sent into the world to preach the good news, and there is no other mission than that of the church of Christ. Preaching, then, is so important because this task is not just one of many other religious activities of the church, but it is the criterion for all its activities. It is exactly by going outside itself to preach that the church is itself and comes to itself.

Importance of Preaching

Second, consider the authority in preaching. A herald in New Testament times was a member of the royal court and a spokesman of a prince or king. These heralds had with them a scepter or royal seal to indicate that what they said was said with the very authority of the king. The Apostles considered themselves as sent by the Lord to communicate in his name a message of life. They were convinced that when they spoke they did it on behalf of King Jesus, and when they did it with integrity it was as if he himself was talking. In 2 Corinthians 5:20, Paul expands this understanding of the mission when he says that we are like Christ's ambassadors, "as though God were making his appeal through us." As witnesses today around the world we need to recover this confidence. We need to grow in the conviction that we are not representing ourselves before the world, but we are facing the world in the name of Christ the Lord and with his authority and power.

Furthermore, the Holy Spirit is promised to all believers to provide the utterance and wisdom we will need as we are involved in mission so that our witness might make an effective contribution to the ongoing redemptive purpose of God (Mark 13:9-13). In this passage Jesus stated that to each one of his people, specific tasks would be given. Together with them, he would also give them the spiritual authority (*exousia*) that they would need in the inevitable cosmic struggle that this worldwide task of preaching the gospel would involve (Mark 13:34).

Power of Preaching

Third, consider the power of preaching. The power that energizes our preaching is double. It comes from the Holy Spirit and it manifests itself through the Word of God when proclaimed in that power. It is this combination of the Spirit and the Word kept in balance, which is our inheritance from the Reformation, that makes Christian preaching the source of good news and reconciliation.

Facing an unbelieving, agnostic and relativistic world, we need to cling not to the power of our eloquence or rhetorical resources but to the power of the Word we proclaim. The "Word of God is living and active" and the Lord says "it will not return to me empty" (Hebrew 4:12, 13; Isaiah 55:11). It is time for us to take this truth seriously and to stand firm before the world and the church with a message that is not the expression of our invectiveness or ingenuity, but "is the power of God for the salvation of everyone who believes," as we read in Romans 1:16.

However, we Baptists have, sometimes, come to believe that there is some sort of magical power in the book. In our commitment to be faithful to the Word of God we have forgotten that the Protestant tenet of *sola scriptura* does not mean that the power of our preaching lies only in the mechanical repetition of the words written in its pages. The source of power is not the book but the Spirit who inspired its message. If our preaching rests only on what the book says without the operation of the Holy Spirit, there is no power or authority in our preaching. Jesus was pretty clear when he said, "The Spirit of the Lord is on me, because he has anointed me to preach."

Proclaimers of Freedom

We should be "proclaimers" or announcers of freedom

Our text says that the Messiah was sent "to proclaim freedom." The Greek verb used here is *keruxai*. This is a very rich action. The verb "to proclaim," *kerussein,* means to publish, to preach. It is used as the verb "to preach the good news," *euaggelisasthai*, appearing some 61 times in the New Testament. The noun "proclamation," *kerygma,* appears eight times and "preacher" or "announcer," *kerux,* only three. The basic idea being conveyed is that of a herald who delivers a message that has been entrusted to him by the king.

In this way, the second element in Jesus' messianic program has to do with the proclamation of freedom to humankind. In a world sunk in dungeons of darkness, with chains binding minds, hearts and hands, we are given the unique task of proclaiming freedom. We are the announcers of a Gospel that is light to quench any dark thoughts; it is love to heal any broken heart; and it is power to release any bondage of sin. As we faithfully proclaim this Gospel of freedom the forces of evil are set back and the kingdom of God is manifested. However, we need to take into consideration three fundamental issues.

First, to proclaim freedom we should be free. I know that most of us with a Calvinistic background in our theology will respond: "Yes, we are free forever and ever." In a sense, this is true. But I am not talking of the doctrine of salvation here but of the doctrine of sanctification. In Jesus Christ we are set free if we repent of our sins and trust in him as our Lord and Savior. However, we need to grow in this freedom, and sometimes it is here where we fail. With our consent, the devil develops all sorts of bindings and oppressions that limit our freedom. The consequence is that the Holy Spirit who dwells in us is grieved and quenched, resisted and cornered in our lives, and we become unable to proclaim freedom to others in his power.

Throughout fifteen years as a Baptist pastor, I used to serve the Lord in the power of the flesh and with increasing bindings entangling my life and ministry. I was a very successful Baptist young leader to others. But I knew I was in trouble. Deep in my heart I knew I was a fake. Finally, totally disappointed, in frustration, depressed and guilty, I decided that the best thing for me to do was to leave the ministry in 1979. I felt that I had no moral or spiritual authority to guide others when I myself was so lost. I knew that I was saved, but my sins did not allow me to grow in Christ and to be filled with the Holy Spirit to serve him with power and authority. It was by his grace, his mighty grace, that on Easter Sunday, 1983, early in the afternoon, the Lord broke the chains that were so tight around my mind, my heart and my will.

I was alone in my bedroom taking a nap. As I was lying down on my bed I began to pray thanking the Lord for his mercy upon me, that in spite of my many sins he continued to use me. And then, in the twinkle of an eye, on the wall in front of me, as if it were on a movie screen, I saw all my sins parading before my eyes. I was paralyzed on the bed and began to cry with desperation as I said, "Forgive me, Lord, forgive me." My heart was broken as tears were flowing from my eyes. I do not know how long this vision lasted, but to my surprise it disappeared when the Lord in audible voice talked to me. In very sweet tones he spoke to me these simple words: "Pablo, I want you to pray for the sick persons tonight." And immediately he gave me names and conditions. I was scheduled to preach that night at Nueva Chicago Baptist Church in Buenos Aires where I served for seven years. I asked permission of the pastor to pray for the sick at the end of the service, and that night I saw miracles happening as never before in my ministry.

After two years in Texas serving at Southwestern Baptist Theological Seminary as the first national guest professor and completing my doctorate, I returned to Argentina to serve as pastor at Central Baptist Church in Buenos Aires. Now I knew the difference between serving the Lord and the church in the power of the flesh and serving in the power of the Spirit. There is a world of a difference between being saved and serving in captivity, and being saved and serving anointed with the Holy Spirit. We cannot be announcers of freedom to others if we ourselves are in captivity.

Second, to proclaim freedom we should be agents of freedom. The salvation that comes through faith in Jesus Christ frees us from our guilty conscience and from our state of condemnation (Romans 8:1-2). The Gospel we proclaim is a Gospel of forgiveness and new life in Christ. To be in Christ means to be filled with the Holy Spirit, and this means to be free from the power of sin and death. When we are filled with the Spirit we enjoy true freedom and we become agents of freedom. Justified and liberated by the Spirit because of our faith in Christ, we are able to dedicate ourselves freely and unconditionally to the cause of justice and freedom. Thus justification and forgiveness, far from being exhausted in the gracious action of a transcendent God, are confirmed by the practice of justice and the liberation of others.

Our experience of justification and liberation from sin is not just a personal spiritual experience that is limited to us. Justification and liberation are not circumscribed to our personal practice of justice and freedom. We are called by our Lord to become his agents of justice and freedom in this conflictive and captive world. In the name of Jesus and with the power of his Holy Spirit we have to go to the world and proclaim and work out freedom in the midst of social injustice, political oppression, economic corruption, religious confusion, and cultural relativism. As agents of freedom we should commit ourselves to the kingdom of God and proclaim liberation from sin, knowing that evil works both in personal life and in exploitative social structures that humiliate humankind, but which can be redeemed in Christ. Our proclamation of freedom should target both the liberation of individual sinners from sin and the liberation of human society from injustice and oppression.

Third, to proclaim freedom we should be servants of Christ. There is no true freedom outside Jesus Christ. He is the Liberator, the Redeemer of all humankind. The only hope of freedom to our world is in him. There is just one way to freedom for any human being, and that rests in becoming servants of Christ. This is the central paradox of the Gospel we proclaim; that in becoming his servants we are able to experience true freedom. And this freedom is produced in us through the work of the Holy Spirit, who dwells in us. As the apostle Paul says: "The Lord is the Spirit, and where the Spirit of the Lord is, there is freedom" (2 Corinthians 3:17).

Besides, we should make our own the *kerygmatic* confession, "Jesus is Lord," knowing that, necessarily, this proclamation of our faith involves a movement outward toward the world as the arena and recipient of the Gospel of the kingdom. However, we should subject ourselves to this confession knowing also that the reconciling, redeeming, and renewing kingdom of our Lord is a universal kingdom that includes all nations.

Let us follow Jesus' steps in our understanding of the mission he has entrusted to us in the world. Let us be preachers of good news and proclaimers of freedom anointed by the Spirit of the Lord to the glory of his name. Amen.

6. Proclamation (Sermon)

Karl Johnson

A dying art that refuses to die; a vanishing practice that refuses to disappear; a devalued calling that refuses to be written off.

What are we talking about? Proclamation! Yes, that to which we refer is the endangered pursuit known as preaching!

Many of us should know by now that preaching has hit upon some extremely turbulent weather in recent years. It seems as if the times in which we live have relegated proclamation, preaching, to its margins. It is seen as a throwback to antiquity as a means of communication; some would banish it to the museums rather than in the midst of our modern age.

Yes, it has been the recipient of bad press both within and outside the church!

It is one thing for the world to dismiss proclamation as being significant only as a relic of the past but it is a totally different thing when we preachers begin to believe this propaganda. Sadly, many of us as preachers have lost, and are losing, confidence in the ministry of preaching and proclamation, especially in this age of media and technology.

But I have news for us and it is that preaching has never lost its efficacy or potency. Far from it!

I stand on the side of those who view proclamation – on the side of those who understand preaching – as a unique ministry grounded in the will and purpose of God in Christ through the witness of the Spirit. In God's wisdom it is the primary way in which the Good News is to be shared in the world. There is simply no authentic equivalent to the fundamental practice of proclamation in human civilization. Indeed, there can be no real and viable substitute for it.

This is so, especially for all those who continue to take their cue from biblical tradition – a cue that all God's true people are expected to take. For in the biblical tradition proclamation is a mandate that is confirmed; a practice that is exemplified; a necessity that is underscored.

Nowhere is this better demonstrated than in the life and experience of the much neglected prophetic pioneer, the eighth century prophet, Amos. From Amos we can learn so much about what God intends his servants to be and do as God's prophets and messengers. And we shall do this by focusing on the eighth verse of the third chapter of Amos, which says, using the New International Version, "The lion has roared, who will not fear? The sovereign Lord has spoken, who can but prophesy?"

Divine Compulsion

When we look at Amos we see **proclamation as a vocation grounded on irrepressible divine compulsion**. He would say, "I did not enter this ministry based on my family heritage or tradition. In fact, as others have said, I am not even one worthy of such a noble tradition. For I was a little unknown man from an equally obscure district in Judah called Tekoa. A place that could easily elicit scornful questions such as 'Can anything good come from Tekoa?' But I had no choice but to respond to the claims of God on my life! The Lord spoke – I could not but proclaim!"

Chapter three of the book of Amos and the first eight verses give us an insight into Amos' self-understanding as he recites a list of questions whose answers are meant to be self-evident. In what can be described as a "cause and effect" rhythm, Amos asks questions such as: "Do two walk together unless they have agreed to do so?" We hear him ask again, "Does a lion roar in the thicket, when he has no prey?" The answer to both is a resounding

"No!"   "When a trumpet sounds in a city, do not the people tremble?" "Yes!"   "The lion has roared", he asks further. "Who will not fear?"   We know the answer – everyone will fear. **The Lord has spoken – who can but prophesy?**   "I had no choice – it was a divine compulsion!"

But Amos would never claim to be unique and/or alone in this experience and today in 2010, with the benefit of hindsight, we know that the scripture is replete with testimonies of this sense of irresistibility when God lays claim, when the Spirit of God seizes an individual to do his bidding. Who can but respond?

It is the same kind of affidavit that we would have heard from the lips of Jeremiah when he said, "If I say, 'I will not mention him or speak any more in his name,' his word is in my heart like a fire, a fire shut up in my bones. I am weary of holding it in, indeed I cannot" (Jeremiah 20:9).

Do we not detect testimony akin to this in the response of Peter and John when they were hauled before the Sanhedrin and commanded to stop preaching in the name of Jesus? They stated unequivocally, "We cannot but proclaim what we have seen and heard!"

Echoing similar sentiments is Paul, formerly known as Saul of Tarsus, who, caught up in a stirring defense of his apostleship, with his integrity and his motive in question, declares, "When I preach the gospel I cannot boast, for I am compelled to preach. Woe to me if I do not preach the Gospel" (1 Cor. 9:16).

These are but a few examples in scripture that attest to what Amos described as an irrepressible compulsion that drives us to obey God, to respond to God, to become God's mouthpiece, to proclaim his word and his mind!

This carries with it an awesome responsibility – a responsibility never to project or present anything or anyone else, save God and the message that God has given to us. Preaching, then, is a dangerous occupation; proclamation is a frightening engagement, as we stand in the name of, and on behalf of, the God of this universe, who chooses to use us as his intermediaries, to speak His word.

Yes, communication skills are important. Technique is important. Homiletical tools are important. But, none measure up, and none are as critical as the message itself.

I proclaim to you, whom God has gathered here in Honolulu from across the world, that it's not more aids - visual, aural or technological that we need. We do not need more oratorical gymnastics; we do not need more lyrical gimmicks; we need more messengers of God, bearers of the word of God, conduits of the truth, of the counsels of Almighty God. Persons who will proclaim, "Thus says the Lord."

And in so saying and doing, we will have opened ourselves; we have disciplined ourselves; we will mean that we have, by God's grace, informed ourselves to know, understand, respond and hence represent the truth that God has entrusted to us. In simple terms, proclamation requires a proper theology, a proper understanding of God.

Such is the awesomeness of this task that we need always to be wary of persons who are overly glib and overly confident in the handling of this truth, for the weight of it rests heavily on us; we dare not misrepresent God!

Persons, under the weight of this mandate should resist every attempt to exploit this responsibility by converting it into a commercial enterprise. Let us eschew, let us turn our backs, on any temptation to prostitute this ministry of proclamation, to construct prerequisites for its execution that will in any way detract from the sovereignty of God, the authenticity of his message and the sheer joy that comes from being obedient to him.

Inescapable Tension

In addition to seeing proclamation as a vocation grounded in irrepressible divine compulsion in Amos' life, **we also see proclamation as a vocation confronted by inescapable tension**.

Speaking with the authority of a man who has "been there, done that," Amos would share with us that once we stand in the name of God, there will be what could be termed certain occupational hazards, some things that "come with the territory." These realities create tension in our lives and in our ministries as we seek to be faithful proclaimers of God's message.

One patently painful thing that confronted Amos could be described as the tension of location.

During Amos' ministry he discovered that there were persons who would seek to discredit and disqualify him by virtue of his origin, by dint of where he came from. He learnt this the hard way when Amaziah, the priest of Bethel, the "head honcho" in religious circles up North, became irritated by his message and recommended strongly that he, Amos, return to his hitherto obscure confines. Amaziah viewed Amos as an outsider as he was preaching in the northern region while he was from the South.

In Amaziah's eyes Amos didn't belong and had no business prophesying in that region as he was a "little" rural, unexposed and unsophisticated man who found himself dabbling in matters beyond his scope and competence.

Amos' response was simple and direct: "I am neither a prophet nor the son of a prophet. I have never been to 'prophet school;' I am but a herdsman – a dresser of sycamore trees. It was the Lord who took me from my business and said, 'Go prophesy!'"

As far as Amos was concerned, his presence in the North was not on account of privilege bestowed by the state; neither was he clothed in the garments of empire or protected by the trappings of the mighty. He was there solely because of his divine vocation. It was God who had sent him!

There may well come times in our lives, in the life of the prophet, of the preacher, when people locate us in boxes of their own choosing and proceed to summarily dismiss us on the basis of where we are from, where we went to school or the part of the world in which we reside. People will dismiss us as inferior, as having no *locus standi*, as having no place *here* because we are not *from here*.

And how could we forget those who elevate themselves as the arbiters and guardians of how theology and enlightenment are to be understood and proceed to dismiss us simply because they view our "location" as "less than."

The fact of the matter is that at times tensions emerge not just because of geography but based on factors such as class, race, gender, politics, and the list is endless.

We who stand in the name of God in Christ Jesus will always face tension in a world that is still upside down concerning matters of equality and notions of superiority. Whatever the source of the tension, let us stand firm in the conviction that we are here, not so much because we think that being here brings with it a sense of actualization, but because we go where God sends us, do what God bids us to do and say what God tells us to say.

And remember this: the strength of our authority does not reside in our sponsors; the force of our message does not depend on the Ivy League, rarefied atmosphere of any institution; our authority comes from God's call on our lives and God's message is never inferior! No one has any superior message based on their origin, based on their location, based on their pedigree, based on their schooling, based on their orientation. God calls and it is God by his Spirit who authenticates!

Let every preacher locate themselves in this reality of the divine vocation – it is God who has sent us, not we ourselves.

Untenable Expectation

In Amos we see further that **proclamation is a vocation that challenges untenable expectation.**

It seems to me that we can get into trouble when we speak truth that people do not expect or think they need. For isn't it true that when Amos was thundering against Damascus in chapter 1:3, against Gaza in chapter 1:6, against Tyre in chapter 1:9, it seems that the Israelites were happy?

Many preachers can recreate that scene – the scene in which you are dealing with certain topics and the congregants are preaching along with you; the church is swinging from the chandeliers with you. But then comes the moment that you begin to touch issues that point to their own shortcomings and their own failures – you move from "hero to zero" with Usain Bolt-like speed!

That's what seemed to have befallen Amos – when he turned to Judah and more so to Israel and started to enumerate their acts of injustice, wickedness against the poor and their general moral failures. They became angry with him; they turned against him. They did not take kindly to being singled out by Amos as persons who should know better than to engage in the practices that marked their lives.

Amos' words challenged any notion they might have had that their status as God's special people meant they could do anything and get away with it! His proclamation shattered their world of complacency by telling them that they had no guaranteed safety.

It was this that angered the priest Amaziah and led him to declare Amos "persona non-grata": "Leave, this is not what we expected you to preach!"

Authentic proclamation so often invites this type of tension and we need preachers who will not consider their bank balance or examine their own welfare before determining what to preach. We need preachers who will not stop to assess their future with congregations and organizations before deciding whether they should obey God in what they say.

We need preachers who, in proclaiming God's truth, will not first and foremost think of their own fate but will be preachers and pastors who will challenge people in their comfort zones, in their shortcomings, in their failures; challenge them saying, "Thus saith the Lord;" calling them to right relationships, to right living; calling them back to God.

One of the painful realities of this divine vocation is that, sometimes, our enemies and strongest opponents are within. They are drawn from those persons who make up the congregations, the organizations that we have been called to serve; they are the ones who want to put words in our mouths or to banish us from their presence.

Yes, there can be no more stinging, biting and gut-wrenching experience than to be attacked from within because when the attack comes from without we can build fences; we can strengthen and fortify our defenses. When it comes from within, however, it can catch us off-guard; it can destabilize us; it can send us cowering into the closet with our backs against the wall, wondering, "My God, my God, why have you forsaken me?"

In moments like those, remember that you did not send yourself, and the God who has called you to proclaim is the God who has promised to protect. It is as we go through experiences like those that portions of Scripture become even more real, personal and pointed to us. A psalm like Psalm 23 serves to remind us of God's providence and protection, no matter what we are going through – Yea though we walk through the valley of the shadow of death we will fear no evil, for God is with us. Surely, goodness and mercy partner us. How we are reminded of the words of Jesus, "Go ... and remember I am with you always." And we know, "If God is for us, who can be against us?"

Is there anything else that Amos would say to us? He would say perhaps one final thing and it is this: **Proclamation is a vocation that, while attending to contextual relevance, maintains a global vision**.

It is able to do this because such is the nature of the God who calls and the God who is proclaimed. Our God is a universal God and we need to ask him to expand our vision of him and to allow us to see him as he truly is.

So, while each of us has a local address, we must remember, as did Amos, that our message, while having contextual relevance, cannot be confined to geographical boundaries. And Amos would say, "I tried to speak to a wider field than just my people; I tried to speak to the centers of influence of my time. I spoke to them, for God had a word for them as well."

Our message is therefore never culture-bound, even though it must have cultural relevance and sensitivity. Our message must never be exhausted only by local concerns.

We who have gathered here must see ourselves not as a motley crew of fanatics or religious sycophants. We are God's people, the universal God is our God and we are huddled here to hear what the Spirit will say to us through God in Jesus Christ. And yes, we have come with openness to respond with obedience to what God has said, and what God will say to us.

Isn't it a fact that the global reach of the Baptist World Alliance, yea the whole church of Jesus Christ, is extended further toward the ends of the earth whenever God's messengers rise to proclaim his truth in Jesus Christ in every nook and cranny, every village and inner-city community, before congregations of less than ten or mega-congregations, in every language known to humankind? Surely there can be no more global approach than "you in your small corner and I in mine!"

Our message, or better yet God's message in Jesus Christ through us, when we leave here will be contextual, but it will not be parochial. Let our message challenge the structures of imprisonment, bondage and evil that are manifesting themselves in sinful ways and acts of rebellion (moral, relational and otherwise) all across this world.

Let us speak truth to power; let us proclaim truth to systems that nourish inequity and injustice, racism and poverty; and let us say with clarity and conviction, without fear or favor, thus saith the Lord, "Let God's people go!"

And if they ask us, yea, when they ask us, from whence have we come? Who are we? Tell them, "We are they who have heard the Lord speaking to us! Yea, Our Lord has spoken, we can only but proclaim!" Amen.

7. Liberation (Bible Study)

Janet Clark

Sometimes, it seems, we have to leave home to "hear the spirit" in a new way.

Sometimes when we are dislocated from our familiar context, a familiar passage of Scripture takes on new meaning. Sometimes, when we're with people from locations, backgrounds, and life experiences that are vastly different from our own, we see things through their eyes that we never saw before. Such has been my experience.

I grew up in a small, monocultural town in a semirural area of Canada, a country that by the world's standards is among the privileged. Not surprisingly, I came to know God and understand Scripture in ways that fit my experience. I knew the text of today's study, Luke 4:18, and as a young woman I found it compelling and inspiring:

The Spirit of the Lord is upon me, because he has anointed me to bring good news to the poor. He has sent me to proclaim release to the captives and recovery of sight to the blind to let the oppressed go free (Luke 4:18).

I wanted the mission of Jesus to be mine too. I went to university, studied counseling and social work, and began my first job as a child welfare worker among the urban poor of Toronto, Canada's largest city, in an area notorious for its wrenching social problems. It was a radical relocation for a small town girl.

A few years later, another relocation occurred. I attended the Urbana Student Missions Conference with about 12,000 other young adults, one of whom is now my husband. I was jolted into a new awareness of the global needs of a desperate world, and I stood to commit myself to God's global mission. The eventual outcome, a few years later, was that I was relocated again, to the exact opposite side of the world from where I grew up, living with my husband and four children in a small village in the interior of Indonesian Borneo, Kalimantan, among people who face some of the most difficult and disadvantaged circumstances I have ever seen. I also met followers of Jesus who trusted God more fully, knew their Bible more thoroughly, practiced hospitality more sacrificially, and faced hardship more courageously than I ever had. Working alongside our Indonesian ministry colleagues, listening to their preaching, glimpsing an understanding of the Gospel through their eyes, I came to see how "located" were many of my own interpretations and perspectives. I sometimes cringe at the memory.

I begin with this personal story to underscore how for all of us, our "location" – our backgrounds and life experiences – provide us with lenses that shape our understanding of God, and God's word. The less aware we are of our biases, the more likely they will subtly influence our understandings. But if we can shift our location, or if we find ourselves utterly dislocated through whatever circumstances, it can often be the trigger for "hearing the Spirit" in a more expansive way.

Sometimes the relocation is geographic, but it need not be. Sometimes we can make an internal shift in location. Sometimes our eyes are opened through interacting with people from different locations, like we are this week. Sometimes, we don't move at all, but the world around us changes dramatically and we find ourselves in a new place and time.

Without question, the world has changed dramatically from the early congresses of the BWA. The so-called "West" is now as urgent a mission field as anywhere – the new periphery. The gravitational center of Christianity has shifted south – to Africa, Asia and Latin America. Some of the most creative theological work is now being done from the perspective of those who formerly were powerless and voiceless – those who were subjects of colonialism, women, racial-ethnic minorities, the burgeoning churches of the Global South. We are now in a world where the old polarities and distinctions do not hold – between sending and receiving countries, benefactors and recipients, developed and undeveloped. Those who liberate others, those in need of liberation.

Yes, the Spirit is blowing in new directions in our world. We have a chance this week in this global gathering of the people from around the world to hear the Spirit afresh. We have a chance to shift location, perhaps even be dislocated by all we hear and experience, but that is the start of new learning.

And so, as we come to this text today, I propose that we approach it from three different locations or perspectives:
1. First, by trying to locate ourselves in the world of the biblical text;
2. Second, by locating ourselves as the people of God called to be agents of liberation;
3. Third, as people in desperate need of our own liberation.

Location I: The World of the Text

Luke is a wonderfully skilled writer who vividly brings to life the scene of this story. What's interesting about Luke is that he was from the educated upper class, a physician, almost certainly a Gentile – someone refined and respected. But over and over again in this gospel, Luke pays particular attention to Jesus' ministry to the poor, to the outcast, to women, to children, to those labeled as sinners. Somehow this aspect of Jesus' message and ministry profoundly impacted Luke and he wants his readers to see it too.

The scene is Jesus' return to his hometown of Nazareth to launch his public ministry. He has been through the wilderness experience and resisted the temptations of gratification, wealth and power. He is ready to give his inaugural address, His personal mission statement.

Luke helps us picture the scene in the synagogue that day: Jesus stands, as was the custom, to read the scroll of the prophet Isaiah (taken from Isaiah 61:1-2 and Isaiah 58:6). He sits to give the interpretation. Luke builds the suspense by telling us, "The eyes of all in the synagogue were fixed upon him" (v. 20). Then the climactic declaration: "Today this scripture has been fulfilled in your hearing" (v. 21).

As we try to locate ourselves in the world of the text, let's attend to four things in particular.

First, Jesus grounds his mission in scripture. Even as he used scripture to respond to the Enemy in the wilderness, he uses scripture to frame his mission and purpose. [We would do well to do likewise]. The Isaiah text would have been known and understood by the listeners that day as a messianic text, a description of the Lord's Anointed One, the promised Messiah. Although there is initial excitement at the announcement that the messianic era is at hand, some take offense and try to run him out of town. It seems that part of the hostility was that Jesus' interpretation of the text is so radically different from their own understandings. They saw the messianic texts as God's covenant with them, the chosen people, not for all. Their interpretations were conditioned by their tradition, their "location," and they couldn't make the shift.

Second, Jesus' ministry is marked by the presence of the Spirit. The Spirit had descended in His baptism by John and had guided him in the wilderness. All that Jesus does in the following chapters is by the power of the Spirit – teaching, preaching, healing, casting out demons, ministering to Jews and Gentiles, women and men, slave and free.

Third, it is absolutely clear in this inaugural mission statement that the "good news" for the poor is not only verbal proclamation, it is accompanied by action: release to the captives, the recovery of sight to the blind, letting the oppressed go free. Jesus' mission is both proclamation and liberation. "Good news" and "good deeds" go hand in hand. The mission of Jesus is holistic. It is "integral mission." The rest of the gospel of Luke is an expanded account of how Jesus goes about accomplishing this integrated mission. Proclamation is corroborated by action.

This is underscored when John sends his disciples to ask Jesus if he is indeed the promised Messiah, or if they should wait for another. Jesus points to the evidence, "Go and tell John what you have seen and heard: the blind receive their sight, the lame walk, the lepers are cleansed, the deaf hear, the dead are raised, the poor have good news brought to them" (Luke 7:22). In sum, Jesus brings liberty, not only proclaims it.

Finally, as the larger context of the text makes clear, the message of liberation is material and spiritual, not one or the other. A study of the way the words are used in the rest of Luke's gospel, and in the whole of scripture, provides sound reason for interpreting these words of liberation multidimensionally.

The poor are most definitely the economically poor, but we also see repeated references in scripture to the "poor and needy" in the spiritual sense of the term.

"Sight for the blind" similarly carries literal and symbolic meaning. Luke records miraculous accounts of physical healing of the blind (e.g. Luke 18:35-43), but elsewhere in this gospel, sight for the blind is a metaphor for the spiritual work of salvation, light to those in darkness, seeing the revelation of God (Luke 1:78-79; 2:29-33; 3:6).

The references to "release" and "freedom" likewise carry both material and spiritual meaning. This imagery of liberation is rooted in the year of Jubilee, when liberty is proclaimed through the land and all debts are cancelled (Lev. 25:8-17). Luke records how Jesus releases persons from various forms of captivity and oppression – physical freedom for the lame, political freedom for the condemned, freedom from the demonic, freedom through the forgiveness of sin. We can call this integral liberation.

What is clear in the text, and amplified in the rest of the gospel, is that Jesus' mission is to make people whole.

His mission was scriptually grounded, spirit annointed, holistically demonstrated and fully integrated.

In the mission of Jesus there is no separation between proclamation and liberation, between evangelism and social concern, between good news and good works. How is it that so often we miss this? How is it that so often in evangelical history and theology, social justice and liberation are seen as secondary, or even a distraction, to the "real work" of evangelism? The two are inseparable. Let us hear the text again for the first time.

Location 2: Let us shift location to the here and now. Let us hear the Spirit's call to be agents of liberation.

In their book, *The Liberating Pulpit*, Justo and Catherine González tell an interesting story that illustrates how social locations influence how people hear and interpret scripture. As part of a seminary course they were teaching, students reflected on the text we are studying today, Luke 4:18-19. Interestingly, they found that white, male seminarians typically interpreted this passage as referring to their own call to ministry. However, women and those from minority groups tended to interpret it differently. Most important to them was that Jesus had been anointed to bring good news to them, to proclaim release to them. The authors observed that those accustomed to privilege tended to identify at one place, while those whose experience was the opposite identified at another.[1]

This is why it's so critical that we intentionally position ourselves in different locations so we can hear the whole Gospel. Both readings are true; either alone is incomplete. This text is directed to all of us, the whole people of God. We are all called to extend the mission of Jesus as agents of liberation. And we all are in need of liberation.

So let us locate ourselves to hear the Spirit's call to us, the church, to extend Christ's mission of proclamation and liberation. This text provides us with a simple but comprehensive framework by which to evaluate our own lives

---

[1] J. González and C. González, *The Liberating Pulpit*. Eugene, Oregon: Wipf & Sock, 1994, p. 84.

and ministries. How are we doing? Are the features of Jesus' mission and ministry reflected in my own life's mission, in the mission my local church, my denomination, in the mission of the BWA? Are we a people known for standing in solidarity with the poor and oppressed? Are we known as advocates for justice and agents of liberation? Are we, the church, the sign and foretaste of God's kingdom reign, pointing to the kingdom that has already come, and forward to the kingdom that is yet to come?

These are not rhetorical questions. I have been asking them of myself and my own context. I'm the dean of a seminary, Tyndale Seminary in Toronto, located in one of the most multicultural cities in the world. And I've been asking myself and the faculty – in what ways does the mission of our seminary reflect the mission of Jesus? Are we known for our commitment to standing in solidarity with the poor and oppressed? Are we as concerned about equipping people for ministries of liberation as much as we are about teaching them the skills of proclamation? Is social justice an integral part of our curriculum, not an addendum to it? We are moving in the right direction, but we must do more.

Ask these questions of your own church, your own organization...your own life.

But even as I challenge us to hear the Spirit's call to be agents of liberation, I must add an accompanying word of caution. There is an inherent danger in setting ourselves up as agents of somebody else's liberation.

Christian history is fraught with horrific examples of the use of supposedly Christian theology not to liberate but oppress – to justify colonization, racism, the ruin of ancient civilizations, the subjugation of women, the forceful removal of aboriginal children from their families and communities, and the list goes on. Often this was done by well-intentioned people who were sincere in their beliefs, but blinded by their locations and perspectives. It is hubris to think that we know better, that we are more enlightened, that we are immune to such error.

So how do we respond to this call to be agents of justice and liberation, but avoid the dangers of perpetuating oppression in the very attempt to alleviate it? Two things are critical.

First, we as the global church must learn how to create partnerships of true mutuality and reciprocity. We need to create a space – a new social location – for interdependence and shared partnership in the mission of God. We must rid ourselves of any notion of the "haves" giving to the "have-nots." We all have something to give; we all come with deficits.

As René Padilla says, this is not a partnership in a contractual sense, but rather as "partners in obedience," who come together by God's will, for the doing of God's will. Because there is one church, one world, and one Gospel, Christian mission cannot be anything other than mission in partnership. The poor and oppressed are not just objects of our charity, but partners in the Gospel. Everyone's voice is needed at the table, each sharing out of what they have.[2]

What does it take to build this kind of partnership in this new era of the global church? An absolutely essential ingredient, says Brazilian pastor and theologian Valdir Steuernagel, is that we learn to listen well. We must learn listening love. This is easy to say but hard to do. It is particularly hard to have money and still listen. As Steurnagel says, "The golden rule seems to be, 'The one who has the gold makes the rules.' "[3]

The challenges of creating this kind of true reciprocal partnership was brought home to me in a recent conversation with a person who heads a ministry for First Nations people (the aboriginal people), one of the poorest and most oppressed groups in my country. A Christian group came to him with lots of money and a plan for how they would help. The longer they talked, the clearer it became that this was not an offer to collaborate

---

[2] C. René. Padilla, *Mission between the Times: Essays on the Kingdom*, Grand Rapids: Eerdmans, 1985.

[3] V. Steuernagel, "More Partners at the Table: Interview by Tim Staffor," *Christianity Today*, January 2010.

together in mission, to listen to the voices of First Nations people about what they most needed, and to recognize the contribution they both could make to a joint project. This First Nations leader did something I find quite extraordinary – he turned down the money. Can you imagine how hard that is when your resources are so few? Liberation means collaboration.

True mutual collaboration in mission also requires that we find partners who will provide both support and critique. I'm not talking about criticism which is cheap, but the capacity to speak truth in love, to critique ideas, to challenge directions, to offer different interpretations from a different location – knowing that there is enough trust in the relationship to bear it.

I suggest that the capacity for mutual critique – not the absence of it – is one of the highest indicators of trust in a relationship. It is dangerous to have partners in mission who try only to please – perhaps because one party needs the other's resources, perhaps because of perceived power differentials, or perhaps out of misguided "cultural sensitivity." The greater the trust, the more we can speak truth, the stronger the bond of partnership.

My greatest hope for the BWA is that together, as the family of Baptist churches from around the world, we create a space for genuine partnership, true reciprocity, mutual critique, deep listening, and shared obedience to the call of God to be agents of liberation.

A second critical aspect of heeding the call to be agents of liberation is to ensure that we embody in our work the inseparability of proclamation and liberation in the mission of God.

For too long the evangelical movement, influenced in large part by the individualistic ethos of the West, has focused on an individualistic Jesus who is concerned primarily with the salvation of individuals. We've focused on the verbal proclamation of the Gospel, with ministries of compassion added along the way. Now, in this new era of the 21st century, we must go one step further and embrace the holistic, integral mission of Jesus by more fully integrating ministries of justice and liberation into a missional understanding of the church. We have begun this journey in the BWA with the establishment of the Freedom and Justice division. It is not an addendum to our core mission but integral to it.

What is fascinating to note, however, is that often those at the forefront of the Christian Justice movement are the younger Christians, across the globe. They are what Gary Haugen calls "the Justice Generation," a generation passionate about justice issues and with little tolerance for a truncated Gospel that does not encompass the call of Christ for liberation of the oppressed.[5] I see this phenomenon in my work with students. They are passionately concerned with issues of poverty, justice, oppression, human trafficking, economic exploitation, and radical discipleship. I am filled with hope that the upcoming generation of Christian leaders will see what my generation often missed – proclamation and liberation are inseparable. Evangelism and social action are inseparable. Debates about which takes priority are futile. As René Padilla says, it's as useless as the effort to understand which is more important –the right or left wing of a plane.[6]

Hear the Spirit's call to be agents of liberation.

Location 3: A third shift in location – Hear the Sprit's call to be liberated

We will miss all that this text has to teach us if we do not locate ourselves in a third position – seeing ourselves as poor, captive, blind and oppressed – for whom these words of liberation are indeed good news of great joy.

For some here today, there is instant identification with this location. Some here have experienced firsthand imprisonment, poverty, racism, persecution, and oppression in many of its forms. As a Baptist family, we acknowledge and honor you. The world is not worthy of you.

---

[5] G. Haugen, *Good News About Injustive: A Witness of Courage in a Hurting World*, Downer's Grove: IVP Book, 2009.

[6] C. Padilla, *op. cit.*

For others, it may require an intentional, internal shift in location to hear this text from a position of vulnerability and need. For the privileged, it is often difficult to recognize one's own complicity in the oppression of others; harder still, to recognize one's own oppression and need for liberation.

This is not to over-spiritualize oppression or to gloss over horrific injustice. But it is to say that all of us here today stand in need of liberation from the forces of evil.

The Spirit's call to liberation is a call to self-examination. So I invite you to read this text not from a location of strength, but from a position of profound weakness and need. It is from a position of weakness that we can join the struggle for radical liberation, not only of others, but of ourselves. As González puts it, once we acknowledge our own need for freedom, we can learn about our own struggle from those whom we charitably tried to help before.[7] We can become teachers and learners together.

Hear the voice of the Spirit offering liberation to you, liberation from those things that right now, in your life, bind you, hold you captive, and keep you from walking boldly into the circumstances God has placed before you. Ask God, even this day, to reveal to you where you need to be liberated. Let this year, 2010, be your year of Jubilee.

Hear the Spirit speaking of our own need for liberation, so that we can live with profound inner freedom no matter what our circumstances, to the glory of God.

Conclusion

The scripture reading read earlier today, Isaiah 58:1-11, casts a soaring vision of true faithfulness, of holistic mission, a vision of what we can do and be.

---

[7] J. González and C. González, *op. cit.*

Is not this the kind of fasting I have chosen:
to loose the chains of injustice and untie the cords of the yoke,
to set the oppressed free and break every yoke?
Is it not to share your food with the hungry and to provide the poor wanderer
with shelter,
when you see the naked, to clothe them,
and not to turn away from your own flesh and blood?
Then your light will break forth like the dawn,
and your healing will quickly appear;
then your righteousness will go before you,
and the glory of the LORD will be your rear guard (Isaiah 58:1-11).

So help us God to be this kind of people, our light breaking forth like the dawn, for your name's sake. Amen

8. Liberation (Sermon)

Alongla Aier

Not long ago, I visited a cousin in her beautiful garden. A little boy came running towards us... I noticed his bright, alert eyes but also his scarred face and arms... "Oh there's more," said my cousin and, lifting his shirt, showed his back covered with scars – zig-zag lines like someone was trying to play tic tac toe with a razor, and then small round scars eaten deep into the flesh... "Cigarette buds," said my cousin. Appalled, I asked, "Who did this?" Then she told his story. His stepfather did it. He was only two when his mother remarried after the boy's father died. For two years he was tortured until he found his new home. Cousin continued, "We've adopted him, named him Joshua... now he even makes up songs: "You are Jesus, mama and papa." This is his way of saying you love me, you're like Jesus.

Little Joshua, now five, has been set free! His spirit can soar as he finds love and acceptance in the home of a family that has embraced him fully.

"The Spirit of the Lord is on me," Jesus read from the Hebrew Scriptures in a synagogue one day. "He has anointed me to preach the good news... He has sent me to proclaim freedom for the prisoners and recovery of sight for the blind, to release the oppressed" (Luke 4:18).

Filled with the power of the Spirit, Jesus was purpose-driven that day in Nazareth; he knew exactly what he was doing. Luke writes that everyone's eyes were focused on him, waiting in suspense – and he declared simply, "Today this scripture is fulfilled in your hearing."

Centuries of waiting have ended. Jesus claims that he is indeed the anointed one, the liberating king, the one scripture foretold! This is the Good News! This good news would totally transform the history of all humankind. Jesus says that the poor, the captives, the oppressed and the blind in particular are the ones to be addressed.

For the people listening to Jesus that day, reference to the poor was not a surprise. The poor were always with them. How were the poor trapped in the vicious cycle of poverty? The main cause was mounting debts! Taxes, tributes, and tolls put heavy pressure on their resources leading to more borrowing, often leading to the poor becoming sharecroppers on their own lands. But God recognizes the poor! The Lord defends the weak and the fatherless and upholds the cause of the poor and the oppressed, defending their rights. It would be foolish to despise the poor, for God is on their side!

Yet, it's not just the economic poor that Jesus was talking about. It is for the pious poor as well. The recognition of one's spiritual poverty is indeed good news. "Blessed are you who are poor, for yours is the kingdom of God" (Luke 6:20)!

Jesus continues reading: "He has sent me to proclaim freedom for the prisoners." Liberation is the main thrust of this good news. For the people listening to Jesus that day, this was no small matter. Memories were awakened and stories were recalled of the struggle of their forefathers and mothers. How could they ever forget Egypt, the years of captivity, the wars that took place over the years, the warnings of captivity, and then the nightmare as women and children, the best of the young men, were taken as captives to alien places. These were awful, painful memories.[1]

"Set the captives free?" That touched a sensitive, still a raw wound for the people listening that day. Weren't they captives of the Romans whose debtors' prison, structures, systems and ideologies had made them servants/slaves in their own land? Oh! To throw off the yoke of Roman rule!

---

[1] See Amos 7:11, I Samuel 30:3, 2 Kings 17:23.

Those listening to Jesus are drawn in, and the Lord keeps reading. "The blind will see!" The folks listening to Jesus hadn't seen anything yet! A quick look at Jesus' ministry and we find that many blind were healed; healing the blind became like a trademark of Jesus' ministry. [2]

They would hear Bartimaeus the blind beggar answer, when Jesus asked, "What do you want me to do for you?" The answer seemed so obvious but Bartimaeus replied in earnestness, "Rabbi, I want to see." And he began to see immediately (Mark 10:46-52)!

Jesus takes the opportunity to draw attention to a radical truth – that blindness went beyond the merely physical. Blindness of the heart and mind are more serious. It represents a hardened heart against God, a stumbling block to God's kingdom. No wonder Jesus said to the Pharisees, "Woe to you blind guides, you blind fools" (Mathew 23: 16-24)!

Liberation! The blind will see! Jesus the light of the world has said, "Whoever follows me will never walk in darkness but will have the light of life" (John 8:12).

"The Spirit of the Lord is upon me ... to release the oppressed." To the slave, the exploited and downtrodden Jesus declares, "I have come to set you free!"

God upholds the cause of the oppressed (Psalm 146:7). God's justice and righteousness are with them. Did he not say, "I have indeed seen the misery of my people, I have heard them crying out because of their slave drivers... So I have come down to rescue them" (Exodus 3:7-8).

Again Jesus is alluding here to more than a literal release from prison. The release he refers to has holistic implications and carries eternal significance. Jesus the Anointed One is here to set prisoners free from all forms of bondage and oppression by sin!

---

[2] Suzii Paynter, "Scriptural Triptych: Announcing the Ministry of Christ," in *This is what a Preacher looks like: Sermons by Baptist Women in Ministry*, Pamela R. Durso, editor, Macon, Georgia: Smyth & Helwys, 2010, p.185.

Madesh was only eight when he was sent to work in a brick kiln. His family was too poor. The work was grueling and dangerous: his task was to mix the clay with his bare feet into a soft paste; he'd get hurt at times – the clay contained broken pieces of glass. For this work Madesh received just a few cents a day for food. He was never allowed to leave the kiln; physically abused, he never experienced the joy of childhood. You see, Madesh was one of twenty-seven million slaves worldwide. For fifteen years he remained trapped in slavery. But the impossible happened. He was released! Thanks to the efforts of a Christian justice group, Madesh and his family are free today. With a little help from others, Madesh has his own brick kiln and now employs people from the community and pays them all fair wages![3] God in Jesus is always moved by the cries of the oppressed and He rescues them.

Coming closer home, how shall we respond to Jesus and His incredible mission? The kingdom work that Jesus declared that day remains unfinished. What can we do? The answer is simple. Get involved! Look around you. More than ever, creation groans for deliverance. The cry of the poor, the blind, the captive and the oppressed is so loud, God's children cannot and should not keep silent! We dare not watch a child die for lack of a cup of powdered milk when even a fraction of our wealth can save millions of children from starvation.[4]

We dare not simply sit and watch the growing millions of displaced people who, like animals, are chased out of their own beloved land. They are not just "refugees." They, too, are made in the image of God and they need help.

We dare not turn a blind eye to the abused, trafficked girls - two million exploited in commercial sex trade each year - when we can lobby, network and influence the powers that are to stop this horror! [5]

---

[3] "Madesh's Story," International Justice Mission, accessed July 1, 2010, http://www.ijm.org/ourwork/southasia.

[4] "State of the World Need," in *Perspectives on the World Christian Movement: A Reader*, Ralph D. Winter, Steven C. Hawthorne, et al., editors, Pasadena, CA: William Carey Library, 1999, p. 574.

[5] "Injustice Today: The Facts," Intenational Justice Mission, accessed July 1, 2010, http://www.ijm.org/ourwork/injusticetoday.

We dare not remain silent and say "no" to the ministry of reconciliation when brothers and sisters of the same faith and race kill each other. Conflicts escalate and the poor, the captives and the oppressed increase in the land!

The challenges are staggering. But there's an underlying challenge that is often ignored or understated. This challenge is to the "non-poor" and the "non-captive." In Jesus' time, the perpetrators remained silent. They sustained the status quo because they benefited from the systems and structures that were in operation.

A tough question to ask ourselves is this: In our position and context, do we, in any way, sustain the status quo that prevents the flow of liberation and justice and keeps the captives still imprisoned? It is said that Christians today have a total annual income of more than one trillion dollars. According to the United Nations, it would cost only $30 - $40 billion per year to provide all people in developing countries with basic education, health care, and clean water. This is the same amount spent on golf every year!

The point is: we have the capacity. If we so decide and act, we can make a difference in our lifetime! How shall we respond?

It is true that the global Baptist family is recognized. We are there, sometimes the first, in crisis situations, in mission and evangelism all over the world. But we are needed more at the cutting edge, for greater challenges for God's Kingdom here on earth!

Do you hear the Spirit? Listen! The same Jesus of Nazareth is here with us, pleading, "Be my hands, my feet, my eyes, and my mouth." Christ has no body on earth. We are his body. By the enabling power and grace of God in Christ, may we respond "YES, in Jesus' name!" Amen.

9. Transformation (Bible Study)

Allan G. Demond

Distinguished guests and friends in Christ, it is a privilege to bring the study from God's word this morning and to express, as I begin, warmest greetings from the land down under – Australia.

As a nation, Australia has a special tie to the theme of this congress. In the early 1600s the Portuguese explorer, Pedro Fernandez de Quiros, declared our nation and region to be: "the great south land of the Holy Spirit." I wish I could report that we had done a wonderful job in the last 400 years; that our whole nation was a vibrant example of the kingdom, that our people feared God and that our text this morning – a call to jubilee – was being lived out all over Australia with exemplary passion. But, I cannot. Alas, ours is a nation like most nations. We have much work to do.

But for just a moment imagine with me if Pedro's words were today's truth. Imagine if there was a place on earth (anywhere really) where God's Spirit breathed righteousness and truth into every word, every action and every decision. Imagine if there was a place where people feared God more than they loved things and they cared for others more than themselves. A place where every citizen confronted injustice and no one was ever complicit with the deep wrongs in our world. Instead of worrying about their possessions and building bigger barns, the citizens of this place would share until no one had a need. Just imagine!

Pedro proclaimed Australia "the great south land of the Holy Spirit" – but as a nation we did not hear it or heed it. Was it just a silly dream? Misguided thinking? When Pedro returned to Madrid in 1607, many regarded him as a "crank," a crazy man, and perhaps he was. Charges of poor leadership and suspected mutiny are in the record against him. But what of his vision – was that nonsense too? Is it only the dreamers who dare say to the nations, God rules here! Is there any hope of transformation?

This brings us to our text and we approach it with a prayer: "Oh God, give us ears to hear the Spirit!"

THE VISION: A Jubilee People

We have just one verse this morning which, in its robust Judaic context makes a jaw dropping claim. Jesus was anointed by God, says the text, "to proclaim the year of the Lord's favor" (Luke 4:19)! So, what is "the year of the Lord's favor?" We can note a few things – theologically, historically and practically.

Theologically it is a big hope-filled idea. The phrase describes a time, acceptable to God, when His salvation will be fully experienced and everything transformed. It is the time when God puts it all right for all eternity! It is the moment that every prisoner, every blind woman, every bound man, every broken-hearted child, every starving family eagerly awaits. It is the ultimate exodus from sin and the final return from exile. It is something to dance about, to write songs and blow horns for, and to shout from the house tops. Theologically, it's a big beautiful idea!

In some ways, the text anticipates Pedro Fernandez de Quiros. Jesus (like Pedro) simply declares the arrival of God's Kingdom. He does not argue the matter but asserts it with mysterious authority. With this inaugural sermon He puts His prophetic stake in the ground. From this point on everything He says and everything He does seems like a trumpet declaring: "The year of the Lord's favor has come!" God's rule is here, and He is about to put everything right.

The challenge with this proclamation – God's Kingdom has come! – is how it makes us feel as we wait. Sometimes I feel like a relative at the airport. I stand waiting for my loved ones to appear at the gate. The doors keep opening and people come through, but not the ones I am waiting for. I feel like this sometimes when I stand in the pulpit and boldly preach: "God's Kingdom has come!" It is like saying: "Oh yes, the plane has landed – I heard the announcement. Jesus the pilot came through those doors and told us so himself! Then he went back into the customs office and we can't see him anymore, but it's coming, his Kingdom is coming!" Whether you are at the airport or in the pulpit you can start to feel the same thing – tired of waiting, anxious and even uncertain. But there is a word from God for every preacher: "Preach on!" There is a word for every worker in the harvest fields of God's kingdom: "The year of the Lord's favor has arrived in Jesus. Wait, wait for the Lord!"

Historically, it was a grand vision of periodic social reform. In Luke 4, Jesus is reading His Bible. He quotes Isaiah (chapter 61) who was in turn referring to the book of Leviticus 25. Here the Hebrew people learned about God's social reform vision – the year of jubilee. The plan was simple: every seven years have a Sabbath Year and rest the fields. Then after every seventh Sabbath year, blow the trumpet and have a jubilee year! This 50th year will be awesome. The people of God will live out the hope of the Kingdom in very practical ways.

The jubilee year would involve three courageous commitments from everyone: (1) leaving the soil to lay fallow, (2) forgiving debts and (3) liberating slaves. These things are revolutionary. Could you imagine the economic and political challenge of such a program? And could you imagine the consequences? Why, it would be like a new earth and a new heaven! It would be like a new Tokyo or a new Mumbai or a new Jerusalem coming down out of heaven.

Someone has calculated that AD 26 would have been the year for a jubilee. If Jesus was born in AD 4 (as many suppose) and if his ministry began at age 30 (Luke 3:23), his inaugural year in public ministry was the calendar year for a jubilee. Jesus was, on this view, a prophet with a deeply exciting agenda calling Israel to social and political reform.

Most scholars agree that Israel never did practice jubilee as a literal program of social reconstruction. So, is Jesus calling his followers to something radical when he announces the arrival of "the year of the Lord's favor?" Theologically it is a big and beautiful idea, a vision of God's righteous rule! But historically jubilee has never been implemented, so what is Jesus saying practically? Does jubilee have continuing importance? Yes, I think it does.

Practically, it is a call to radical discipleship. The Anglican scholar, Nicholas Thomas Wright, argues that Jesus wanted his disciples to live the jubilee model in their gathered life whether the rest of Israel was willing to do it or not. They would become the new Israel, the new hope, the new Adams and Eves. And here I think is the real power of the jubilee proclamation for you and me. Am I willing to live this Luke 4 sermon of Jesus? Are the Christians who form a church together with me in Australia willing to be such a people? Are all of us – Baptists of the world, together with our fellow Christians from many churches around the globe – ready to live lives that say, the year of the Lord's favor has indeed come? Against politics and social norms that look so embedded and unchangeable, are we ready to practice a new way of life in new communities of hope? Are we ready to be jubilee people?

The courageous commitments of jubilee – (1) not planting the fields, (2) forgiving debts and (3) liberating slaves – can be seen to have impacted the ministry and teaching of Jesus and the life of the early church. Jesus has inaugurated jubilee communities. These commitments may seem like distant ideals at first glance, but the principles are remarkably contemporary. They still define radical discipleship in the twenty-first century. Let's consider each commitment briefly.

Resting the Land

It is not hard to imagine a farmer's worries. "If we don't plant, we don't harvest. And if we don't harvest, we don't have provisions. And if we don't have provisions, will we survive?" God says: "Yes!" It will be the season of divine favor. Remember God's provision in the wilderness? God cared for Israel providing enough manna every Friday to feed them through Sabbath until Sunday when he rained down manna again. The jubilee year will be the same. God will provide.

Consider Jesus' promise to you: "Do not set your heart on what you will eat or drink; do not worry about it. For the pagan world runs after all such things, and your Father knows that you need them. But seek his kingdom, and these things will be given to you as well." (Luke 12:29-31; Compare Leviticus 25:20-21). The God of the jubilee will sustain his jubilee people.

Most of us are not farmers and we will not plant a field this year. But, many of us will go to work next week and we will be tempted to think that our livelihood depends on our job security and the next promotion. Well, it isn't true. What would happen if you reduced your income to take up God's call to mission? Do you trust God that much? What would happen if you took leave (without pay?) to serve as a short term missionary? The jubilee principle says that God would take care of you. Do you and I dare believe it?

So if we are going to be jubilee people we will need to trust God, not our capacity to earn or work or be self-sufficient. Jubilee people experience the Lord's favor, because they position themselves to need it!

Forgiving Debts

Jesus' model prayer (Luke 11:1-4) can be read as a jubilee prayer. "Give us each day our daily bread," alludes again to resting the land. And the phrase, "forgive us our debts, as we forgive everyone who is indebted to us," speaks broadly of sin but specifically of financial debt. On this reading, the prayer is a celebration of God's forgiveness and a promise of jubilee attitudes among the followers of Jesus.

Jesus' parable of the unmerciful servant (Matthew 18:23-35) tells us how not to live. The master forgave a large debt and then, almost immediately, the forgiven servant refused to waive a small debt. His selfish actions were judged very harshly. No one who possesses a miserable-minded attitude like that selfish servant can be a true follower of Jesus.

And then there is the opposite, the positive example of Barnabas. He was a man who loved God, the church, and those in need. He sold personal property so he could put money at the Apostles disposal to meet the needs of others. And he was not the only one, according to Acts 4:34 (also 2:45). Leviticus 25 speaks of redistributing the land in the year of jubilee to achieve justice.

If we are going to be jubilee people we will need to be generous. We will consider others before we consider ourselves and yield our resources to the work of God's kingdom. We won't build bigger barns for our extra "stuff;" we will build a new world!

Liberating Slaves

The long shadow of Roman rule that fell across Jesus' homeland of Palestine had enormous financial and social consequences. Many peasants were systematically reduced to poverty, then insolvency and at last slavery. Unable to meet the demands of taxation they were ground into objects of servitude, cogs in the machine.

Some in Israel positioned themselves to reap benefits from this dysfunction. People like Matthew and Zacchaeus became tax collectors and as such they could become very wealthy while others became indebted to them. When they met Jesus, the changes in their lives modeled what jubilee means for people like us.

Jesus visited Zacchaeus and changed his whole perspective. Zacchaeus paid back what he should not have taken, and then he gave half his wealth to address need. Effectively he was a first century Bono establishing the Jericho "Make Poverty History" foundation in the name of Jesus.

Jubilee people confront the system. They take practical steps to address their complicity in the wrongs of society. They use fair-trade products, stand up against poverty, confront injustice with their own resources and seek to obey when Jesus confronts them. Jubilee people lift rocks to see what is underneath – even if they would rather not know that there are more slaves alive today than in Wilberforce's day and that the cheap clothes and tech gear came from a sweatshop with forced child labor. Jubilee people don't get everything right, but they don't bury their heads in the sand either. They listen to hear the Spirit and then they act!

So there is our pattern: (1) a people who trust God to provide for us (not our fields); (2) who are ridiculously generous and share so that none in our community are in need (debts are paid); and (3) who refuse to be part of the system that crushes the weak but instead strive to liberate the oppressed. This is who Jubilee People are.

The vision is wonderful. It always has been. Deep, profound and lasting transformation! But can we make it happen? Is jubilee real? Who dares blow the trumpet?

THE POWER: A Risen Savior

The most significant thing here is not the vision, it is the vision caster! Not only is he the most faithful jubilee person who ever lived, but when Jesus dies and rises again he proves himself to be the one who has the power to make jubilee possible. He is its Lord and King. When he says, "Today this scripture is fulfilled in your hearing," he puts himself at the center of the jubilee vision as its author and finisher.

Many people have some kind of jubilee aspiration. Whether Christians or non-Christians, they have a deep desire to make the world a better place. The followers of Jesus can join them in many different ways. We can share resources, ideas, advocacy and passion. But there is something distinct about our commitment as jubilee people; it is the prominence of Jesus. We know him to be the center of everything and that is why we call him Lord! Without him there is no Kingdom of God, just a long empty wait.

We are so convinced of this that no other name will do and no other leader will suffice. He is our alpha and omega, our first and last.

- It is his grace that changes people from the inside out.
- It is his call to repentance and offer of forgiveness that redefines life
- It is his example that inspires.
- It is his strength that enables.
- It is his presence that builds confidence and courage in jubilee people.
- It is his gift of the Holy Spirit that bends the rules of the universe, filling faithful followers with power.
- It is his resurrection that makes decay and death like temporary interruptions in serious jubilee work.
- It is his name that brings the power brokers and conspirators of the present age to their knees.
- It is Jesus Christ who makes jubilee possible.

If you would be a jubilee person, if you would hear the sermon in Luke chapter four and obey it, then see the preacher in Luke four and follow Him! Jesus, our risen Savior, is the power of jubilee.

Bruce's Story

I have a friend, Bruce. He is a former policeman and a retired pastor who spends two days each week in the inner city of Melbourne witnessing on the streets. He understands the vision and the power of Jesus' sermon in Luke chapter four and he lives it.

Street witnessing is not easy work. Bruce has to trust God in every conversation and he does more than just talk. He brings people along to "Dinner Tonite" – the weekly meal at our church for the hungry and lonely. He connects people with our care ministries. He organizes counseling, food parcels and occasional loans of money for those with challenges. He folds people into small groups and leads Bible studies with inquirers. He advocates for the needy and confronts injustice. In short, he is a jubilee person.

Bruce is a good man doing good work, but what makes his ministry truly significant is the power of our risen Savior working through him. Recently he had a remarkable – somewhat comical – spiritual confrontation in Swanston

Street in Melbourne. It reminded all of us that God is marvelously and mysteriously in charge. It is his jubilee and the name of Jesus will prevail.

Bruce fell into conversation with a Hare Krishna devotee who declared: "All religions are the same." Bruce disagreed, challenging him with the claims of Jesus. After a short exchange, his conversation partner, wanting to end the discussion, pronounced the words "Hare Krishna" upon Bruce as if to invoke an Eastern blessing. Not wanting this to be the last word, Bruce spoke the name "Jesus Christ" over him. The other man said again: "Hare Krishna" and Bruce said: "Jesus Christ." This exchange continued amid the throng of people for what seemed to Bruce like an eternity – an old gray-headed Aussie grappling nose to nose with a partly-shaven pig-tailed young Hare Krishna. It was a laughable sight but a serious confrontation. Bruce thought to himself: "What have we started, I can't let him win. I wonder how long this will continue." He began to pray along the lines of Acts 4:12 acknowledging, "There is no other name under heaven given to men by which we must be saved." The Hare Krishna kept chanting his mantra while trying to pass out literature and Bruce kept praying the name of Jesus maintaining the position of his nose about two feet directly in front of his saffron-robed friend and mirroring his every movement. Calls for support from a circle of waiting, watching, laughing Hare Krishna friends proved fruitless.

Bruce asked God for help and suddenly the phrase, "the blood of the Lamb," (Rev 21:11) popped into his head. He prayed aloud, "Lord, by the blood of Jesus Christ, bind Satan and release this man into a personal relationship with you." To everyone's astonishment the Hare Krishna immediately spoke the name, "Jesus Christ." He was momentarily flabbergasted by the words of his own mouth and so was Bruce. He stopped chanting, and with genuine curiosity asked, "Why don't Christians chant the name of Jesus in the streets like we chant Hare Krishna?" Bruce replied with true Christian compassion, "My concern is that you would know the love of Jesus and experience his power." It is not the syllables of His name but the gift of His grace and the power of His resurrection that drives our mission. Having handed out the last of his cards, the Hare Krishna fled, calling out with a weakened voice, "Hare Krishna." Bruce responded one last time, "Jesus Christ." And it was the last word!

The story is a small reminder of a huge truth. Jesus is Lord! Let it be known that His name is above all names. Let it be known that His Kingdom has come. Let it be known that we, His people, have seen the jubilee arriving, we are working to advance it and waiting to celebrate its full and final completion. We have a vision to be a jubilee people – trusting God fully, living generously and challenging injustice everywhere. And we have the power of Jesus, our risen Savior – power to confront the darkness of this world, power to prevail, power to be faithful, power to live the vision of jubilee and change the world.

Blow the trumpet, sound the horns; the year of the Lord's favor is here!

10. Transformation (Sermon)

Paul Msiza

I am so humbled and challenged to stand on this high podium amongst great preachers, theologians, Bible teachers and this wonderful crowd of Baptist family from all over the world, to do the most challenging task on earth, which is bring the message from Almighty God. But the most challenging task is to bring a message about the Holy Spirit to Baptists. I therefore invite you to pray for me as I seek to present the message. On a lighter note, I hope most of us have not come to this congress buckled with Baptist safety belts or Baptist earplugs, because we do not want to be influenced by a teaching that seems to be leaning toward the Pentecostal and Charismatic movements.

The reality is that we are gathered here as Baptists from all over the world to listen to what the Spirit is saying to the churches under the theme "Hear the Spirit." It is not a choice to "Hear the Spirit," but it is a command from God that says: "He, who has an ear, let him hear what the Spirit says to the churches" (Revelation 2:7, 17, 29; 3:6, 13, 22). The word of God speaks very emphatically that the Spirit is speaking to the church and the church ought to hear what the Spirit is saying today.

Our text for this congress is Luke 4:18-19: "The Spirit of the Lord is upon me, because he has anointed me to proclaim good news to the poor. He has sent me to proclaim liberty to the captives and recovering of sight to the blind, to set at liberty those who are oppressed, to proclaim the year of the Lord's favor" (English Standard Version).

The Lord quoted the words by the prophet Isaiah that "the Spirit of the Lord is upon me for he has anointed me." I pray that the Spirit be upon us today and anoint us to hear what he says to the church today. I will be focusing on the topic, "Transformation."

The word transformation means a change or a conversion or an improvement. This change, conversion, improvement or transformation is a result of an action done to something. That means a change or a conversion does not occur without some action being executed. The Lord Jesus says: "The Spirit is upon me for he has anointed me to proclaim." The proclamation of the word leads to transformation. This is a transformation directed at the poor, the broken-hearted, the captives, the blind and the oppressed. Christ says that because the Spirit of the Lord was upon him then transformation will take place. People's lives will be changed. Because the Spirit of the Lord is upon him there is hope for the poor, the blind, the oppressed and the prisoners. There is hope for all of us. Christ was addressing this to all people of the world. At times we may think this text is not including us because we are people of the church or the born again ones. But we are included among the poor, the broken-hearted, the captives, the blind and the oppressed. Very often we do not see ourselves as being the poor, the broken-hearted, the captives, the blind and the oppressed. The truth is that we are. That is why the Spirit is still at work even today among us. When we hear the Spirit of the Lord, he will convict us and show us that we need the transformation.

Through God's help I wish to focus on two points. The first point is: the true transformation of our lives is the work of the Holy Spirit alone. Secondly, this transformation is a lifetime experience and not a once off happening.

1. The Holy Spirit brings transformation in our lives

The text says, "The Spirit of the Lord is upon me, because he has anointed me." It is the Spirit that brings about the true transformation in our lives. People can still experience some form of transformation outside the influence of the Spirit of the Lord. But from a Christian belief, that kind of change does not bring about redemption. I am talking about a transformation that brings redemption of the lives of individuals, communities and the whole creation. We believe that God is in charge of our lives and there is no other greater force or power outside God's power that can influence our lives in a positive way. It is the Spirit of the Lord alone that brings transformation of our lives. In the Holy Scriptures, both the Old Testament and the New Testament, we read about the transformation of a number of individuals. For example, Moses was transformed from being a fugitive running away from Pharaoh to being a liberator of the people of Israel. The timid Joshua was transformed into a leader and a conqueror. Rahab was transformed from prostitution to a wife and mother to a blessed generation. The fearful Gideon was transformed into a warrior and a worshipper of God. Peter was changed from an ordinary fisherman from Galilee into a great preacher and apostle of the Lord. Paul, a Pharisee full of self-righteousness, was converted into a humble but great apostle to the Gentiles.

These peoples' journey of transformation came through their encounter with God. It is only the Holy Spirit that can bring about that transformation from being captive to being liberated. It is the Holy Spirit alone that can liberate us from being slaves to sin, to ideologies, to myths, to destructive cultures and traditions of men. Religion alone cannot bring about transformation. In the Old Testament, God laments over a religion that is without the Spirit. Isaiah the prophet rebuked the people for fasting while oppressing their fellow worshippers (58:1-8). He rebuked them because their worship did not speak to their daily living. Christ told the Samaritan woman that God is Spirit and his worshippers must worship in Spirit and in truth (John 4:24). Let us hear the Spirit of Lord because it is only he that can open our spiritual eyes, break the chains of oppression and open the prison doors.

The transformation that is by the Spirit transcends all human barriers, because it is done by the Spirit of God and not by people. This kind of change goes beyond race, gender, creed and geographical boundaries. When transformation takes place it doesn't matter whether we are black or white, young or old, male or female, Jew or Gentile. The Spirit of the Lord works the same transformation in all who hear the Spirit. Paul said in Galatians 3:28, "There is neither Jew nor Greek, slave nor free, male nor female for we are all one in Christ Jesus." Those who are transformed by the Spirit have that freedom in Christ. We need the transformation today.

This transformation brings good news to the poor. This world is full of poor people. We are either poor in material things or poor in spirit. The Lord mentioned the poor without defining any kind of poverty he was referring to. The good news is to the poor in general regardless of their situation. The Spirit of the Lord brings hope and transformation for the poor. Every year the G8 (eight richest countries in the world) meet to discuss, among others things, the challenges facing this world. One of the discussion points on the agenda is the Millennium Development Goal relating to poverty alleviation. It would seem that the more they speak and set up goals to reduce poverty, the more the world sinks into serious poverty. It becomes clear that spiritual poverty exacerbates material poverty, because those who are rich materially but poor spiritually usually fail to share with others. I am not here with bad news, but I want to say that there is good news and hope because the Spirit is here and, according to 2 Corinthians 3:17, where the Spirit of the Lord is, there is liberty.

The greatest thing that holds the world captive is sin. Sin brings blindness to the truth, oppression of the weak and suffering of God's people. These are too deep a challenge to be resolved through human strength. We need divine intervention by the Spirit of the Lord to break the yoke of sin, unlock the shackles of suffering and to open the prison doors. Some of those prisons were created by us in the form of traditions, cultures and prejudice. But those of us who believed the Gospel have been set free and filled with the Spirit to become agents of transformation. Through us the Spirit of the Lord still brings transformation to the lives of people. The church was born through the Spirit and is sustained by the same Spirit. Therefore, the ministry of the church is to be used by the Spirit of the Lord to transform individuals, communities and world systems.

2. Transformation is an ongoing business

We experience transformation when we are converted to Christianity, when we accept the Lord Jesus Christ as our Savior and Lord. The Lord said to Nicodemus in John 3:5-6, "I tell you the truth, no one can enter the kingdom of God unless he is born of water and the Spirit. Flesh gives birth to flesh, but the Spirit gives birth to the spirit" (NIV). Every Christian is born again through the Holy Spirit. The Holy Spirit transforms our lives from the kingdom of darkness into the kingdom of light, from hopelessness to a life full of hope and faith. The Spirit of the Lord has opened our eyes so that we may see the grace of God that is in Jesus Christ our Lord and Savior. The Holy Spirit started us on a new journey of life. We were transformed from a road that leads to destruction to a new highway that leads to life eternal.

This transformation does not stop at conversion when we accept Christ to be our Lord and Savior. This is just the first step in our Christian journey. The transformation goes beyond conversion. The Holy Spirit is always at work in the lives of believers. The Spirit continues to transform our lives, moving us from being converts to becoming disciples. When transformation ceases in our lives, then discipleship and growth ceases. When we stop hearing the Spirit, we stop growing in our relationship with Christ. When we stop hearing the voice of the Spirit, our lives become stagnant and we begin to drift away from the light and go back into darkness. We may still go to church and do all that is required in the church, but become disobedient to God. When we stop hearing the voice of the Spirit, our worship becomes a tradition that we control and manipulate. That is why we still find racism, tribalism, and oppression of women and children within the community of believers. We need to hear the Spirit so that we can be conscious of his work in our lives so that we can respond positively. Even though we are converted to Christianity, we still remain weak and fallible human beings who need God's grace daily.

Brian Gaybba, a renowned South African theologian, contends that the transformation by the Holy Spirit impacts the whole creation. "Sin has turned our world into a place that reflects our selfishness and is therefore hostile to us, a place that frequently frustrates us and hurts us as we struggle to live, especially to live happily."[1] Gaybba says that our transformation brings harmony between us and our environment. We are facing the challenge of global warming which is causing enormous human suffering on earth. When we stop hearing the voice of the Spirit and become selfish and arrogant, our lives become destructive even to the environment that God gave to us to live in happily.[1] We need the transformation by the Spirit.

This transformation brings a witness for Christ. It creates harmony within the community of believers. The harmony or unity of the Spirit brings growth because people will see the love of Christ in action. This is good news to all who hear the Spirit. There are millions of people that need to come to Christ and many of them are going to come to Christ through our witness. Our witness is stronger when the Holy Spirit is at work in our lives. Christ said, "I do not leave you alone" (John 14:18). He has sent us the Spirit. I thank God that the Spirit of the Lord is here. He is in charge of us. God said through the prophet Joel: "It shall come to pass afterwards that I will pour out my Spirit upon all flesh. Your sons and daughters shall prophesy" (2:28). The Spirit is here. Christ said, "I must go to the Father so that the Comforter should come" (John 16:7). He said I will go to my Father and ask him to send you the Comforter.

My Bible tells me that indeed Christ has gone back to the Father, because he came and was crucified for our sins. He bled and died on the cross for our transgressions and he was buried in a tomb that belonged to Joseph of Arimathea. On the third day, he rose from the dead. He appeared to many and after forty days he ascended to the Father. On the day of Pentecost the promise of the Spirit came to pass. There was a rushing mighty wind as the Spirit descended upon the earth. He is here today. Hear the voice of the Spirit. Amen.

---

[1] Brian Gaybba, *The Spirit of Love: Theology of the Holy Spirit*, London: Geoffrey Chapman, 1987, p. 260.

11. Dedication (Sermon)

Lance Watson

All praise, honor and glory to God from whom all blessings flow. To our president, our program chair, all of the official family of the 20th Baptist World Congress, to all of the presenters and proclaimers, pastors and leaders, musicians and singers that have preceded us, and to every member of my international Baptist family.

I must express my august gratitude to the president and to our program chair for this kind and coveted invitation to share in this significant moment. I also have to thank my lovely wife and the wonderful members of the Saint Paul's Baptist Church of Richmond, Virginia, who have traveled 4,833 miles to support us and all the members of the Virginia Baptist delegation who have assembled.

I have cells of sympathy scattered throughout this room because I am an African American Baptist preacher and I have brothers and sisters here who know that as an African American Baptist preacher, I am not accustomed to being given assignments or timeframes when I speak and I'm even less accustomed to doing what I'm asked to do, but I won't be long because I've been practicing a new beatitude that goes, "Blessed are the brief, for they will be invited back."

The story presented in Acts 3:1-6 dramatically demonstrates the power of the church under the influence of the Holy Spirit to change handicaps into happy helpfulness; to change disadvantages into delightful deliverances; to change lingering lameness into leaping love. Here is a tragedy that the church full of the Holy Spirit turned into the triumph of amazing grace.

It is the business and mission of the church to make a difference in the world. This pericope describes the first recorded deed that the church performed after its birth on Pentecost; after cloven tongues of fire fell from heaven; after they spoke ecstatically in new languages they had never learned; after they had received the blessed gift of the Holy Spirit whose special work was and is to glorify God and magnify Christ.

The church found a crippled man who had never walked a day in his life and left him walking, leaping and praising God. It is the Pentecostal challenge of the church and to the church to make people, conditions and the world better than they are. The Pentecostal effects of true religion are not merely vertical, personal and spiritual, but horizontal, political, communal and cosmic. The power of the Holy Spirit is not only to make you feel happy and look holy, but also to make you more humane and more helpful in the struggle to make life better.

When God was ready to reveal Godself, to demonstrate how high and holy God is, God showed the world how human and helpful God could become. "The Word was made flesh and dwelt among us, full of grace and truth." Full of reliability and credibility, full of transforming deeds and delightful liberations.

When Jesus saw sickness, he healed it. When Jesus saw hunger, he handled it. When Jesus saw wrong, he made it right. When Jesus saw death, he reversed it. Wonderful changes manifest through the power of God working on and in the plight of humanity.

As we comb the context of this captivating chronicle, we discover Peter and John going up to the temple at the time of prayer as a crippled man was carried to the temple gate called Beautiful, where he was put every day to beg from those going into the temple courts.

Here is a description of the time, place and characters of this immortal story. It was three o'clock in the afternoon; an hour that had special meaning for Peter and John that others disconnected from the cruxifixion of Christ would not recognize.

This hour was the appointed time for the evening prayer and sacrifice in the Jewish temple. At three o'clock in the afternoon, one could see the faithful and free making their way to the holy temple to offer their sacrifice and lift up their prayers to God.

The place was the temple, the house of prayer, beautiful with golden dome and beautiful gates. The people in the spotlight were Peter and John, people of prayer, people who had walked with Jesus, seen him crucified, buried, risen, taken up into heaven and come back down again in the gift of the Holy Spirit on the day of Pentecost.

Peter and John had come straight from the Upper Room where Pentecost had just happened to the temple in Jerusalem at the hour of prayer. Why in the world did Peter and John need to go into the temple after having already been in the Upper Room where they had received the gift of the Holy Spirit and been filled to overflowing with a heavenly anointing? Why did they go?

They were already filled, yet they were craving for more. More grace, not just to enjoy, but to share. More love, not just to receive, but to give. More power, not just to consume, but to channel and communicate to others. More joy, not just to feel, but to impart.

The best religion is expressed in regular, daily disciplines of duty, not just occasional overwhelming spurts of ethereal ecstasy. It is easy to mistake the purpose of God's amazing grace. It is easy to neglect the regular, daily disciplines of duty and when you do: you will leap with excitement, but fail to walk by faith. You will shout in celebration, but fail to serve in commitment. Life in the Spirit of God is not just stepping from peak to peak, but it's stooping down from our mountain of inspiration to the deep valleys of human need. It's rolling up our sleeves, signing up for service, getting off our seat, standing on our feet, functioning under the unction and getting involved with hurting humans. That is exactly what we discover Peter and John doing in this text: they looked at an ugly sight at the Beautiful Gate.

Although they were limited by their own cultural specifications, linguistic and theological presuppositions and ethnic conditions: they were about to be energized by the Holy Spirit to leap across boundaries, break down walls, knock down barriers and open the doors of the church to Greeks, Romans, Africans, women, children and anybody who would accept the amazing grace available in Jesus Christ.

Peter and John went to the temple to get more grace and suddenly discovered a man in need of the grace that they already had. It is important for us to realize that all of our chances to get more come to us wrapped as opportunities to give more. Peter and John went up to get and found a challenge to give.

Here is a man crippled from birth, born handicapped, unable to stand or walk. He could put no weight at all on his feet. He had no use at all of his legs. Some people are born on the underside of privilege and opportunity. Born poor and disadvantaged, born hated and dependent, born rejected and mired deep in poverty and misery. Disenfranchised, disinherited and dispossessed.

The text talks about a man born in the first century AD, but in 2010 scattered all across the globe are people who are as helpless and hopeless as this man. Born disqualified, victimized, crippled by circumstance, condemned by color, cursed by condition. Born to die too soon.

Here is a full-grown man over 40 years old who had never walked or worked a day in his life being carried to the temple called Beautiful to beg for handouts. This man, handicapped by biological happenstance and crippled by cruel circumstance, was out of the game because he had never been in the game. The man could not even get about on crutches, but was totally dependent on others: he had to be carried.

Tragically, that is true of so many people that show up at church: they have to be carried. They are carried on the membership roll of our churches and never heard from again until they are carried into the church for their funeral. Carried, they make no contribution. Carried, they lift up no prayers. Carried, they offer no contributions. They cannot lift, so they lean. They will not help, so they hinder. They are lame, immobile and inactive.

That's why when the roll is called for those who will give, many sit glued to their seat. That's why when the call goes out for those who will serve, so many are never available. That's why when it's time to sacrifice for the cause of Christ, many people look the other way. They are lame, impotent, loveless, useless and spiritually impotent.

No sermon can change them. No song can move them. No Scripture can correct them. No prayer can inspire them. No speech can convert them. No appeal can sway them because they are physically and externally suave, but they are spiritually and internally lame.

It takes more than physical and material beauty to render a spiritual service. Often it is not that we are physically handicapped or fiscally bankrupt, but we are spiritually lame. We cannot do a spiritual work without spiritual power. You can't stand up by yourself. You can't step out on your own. I am lame. You are lame. We are lame until we are spiritually healed and totally transformed by Jesus Christ.

Our fears will frustrate our faith. Our handicaps will hold us back. Our selfishness will strangle our generosity. Our reservations will cancel out our revelations. Our despair will deprecate our diligence until Christ changes us on the inside.

If you don't believe me, just try it. Try to sacrificially support the ministry without being consecrated; try to preach without prayer; try to teach without truth; try to pray without the Holy Spirit; try to sing without the anointing; try to visit the sick or serve the poor on your strength alone. You can't do it.

You can't serve God, sing to God, sacrifice to God, please God, walk with God, praise God or preach God without God. But as we hear the Spirit and yield to the Spirit, we are brought fully and completely into a positive, wonderful, liberating, transformative relationship with God.

We can know God profoundly, feel God deeply, experience God fully and enjoy God genuinely. We are filled with God's Spirit, blessed by God's goodness, lost in God's love, energized by God's goodness, lifted by God's mercy, useful in God's plan and active in God's service.

Look at this lame man – an ugly sight at a beautiful gate. Notice that this miracle did not happen in the temple, but outside the temple. The church does not exist for itself, but it lives in order to improve conditions in the world. It is necessary, but not sufficient, to beautify and build buildings. We have a charge to keep, a God to glorify and a work to do.

Cripples are stranded at the door of the temple. The homeless, hungry, diseased and desperate roam our streets. This man was crippled, but he was *not* dumb. He knew that what was going on *in* the temple should help him *outside* the temple. The supreme test of the effectiveness of what happens in the temple is what happens beyond the temple because of what's going on in the temple.

Therefore, this man chose to lie on his pallet and beg *not* at the gate of the university because academic pursuits are sometimes deaf to the anguished cries of human distress. *Not* at the gate of government because it can be cold, compassionless and indifferent to the problems and pain of the disadvantaged. *Not* at the gate of politicians who have to check the polls to ensure that what they do is politically correct. But this crippled, paralyzed, handicapped, helpless man was wise enough to lie at the gate of the house of God.

He knew that if anybody would help him, it would have to be somebody who had been in the presence of God and it just so happened that Peter and John were going up to the church to worship while the man was being carried to the temple to beg.

Peter and John saw his helplessness; he saw their piety. He did not know who they were, where they had been or the content of their theology or their recent transformative Pentecostal experience.

The world does not know about our religious experience. The culture does not know that we have been with Jesus and been saved by amazing grace.

The man did not know that Peter and John had heard the Spirit speak.

The shouting was over and the challenge of faith was about to begin. The world will not know who we are until we show them by our love. Verse three tells us of their confrontation, "When he saw Peter and John about to enter, he asked them for money. Peter looked straight at him, as did John. Then Peter said, 'Look at us!' So the man gave them his attention, expecting to get something from them."

The man begged for a handout without even looking carefully at his would-be benefactors. He saw them only as potential sources of revenue, but did not look carefully in their faces. He did not notice anything particular about them and we see many people that we never really notice, never really look at and never truly understand.

Sin will make you *see* people without looking at them and *use* people without loving them, but now contrast and compare how Peter and John saw the man. They fastened their eyes on the man. They looked straight at the man as if nothing in the world mattered except this man. They gave him their undivided, unbroken and unabridged Holy Ghost attention.

God will not allow you and me to look up to God without giving us a heart to look out at humanity. Peter and John did not look past the man; they looked straight at the man. So often, we do just the opposite. We look past the pain, suffering, affliction, neglect, poverty, hunger, racism, sexism, ageism, abuse and addiction. Karl Barth once said, "Christians ought to read the Bible in one hand and the newspaper in the other."

Look up to God to receive power and then reach out to hurting humanity to share love. Don't be ignorant of the hurts of humanity – God wants to use us to change it. God wants to hook up holy power on the inside with horrible problems on the outside.

Peter and John studied this helpless man. They looked straight at him. They fastened their eyes on him. They could have been staring up in the sky, but they were looking at the man. They had holy things to study. They had higher things to think about — hermeneutics, eschatology, demonology, anthropology, pneumatology, soteriology, demythology.

They had heavenly things to figure out, theological theories to construct, cosmic things to consider, but they looked straight at the critical mess of a man on the ground. They had just been talking about holy things.

They had just been talking about Jesus and the Resurrection. They had just been talking about Pentecost and the gift of the Holy Spirit. They had just been talking about Peter and his newfound power. They had just been talking about the church and its global mission. About the kingdom and its inevitable growth. About truth and its liberating power. About love and its unquenchable fire. They could have gone past the man. He wasn't an attractive sight. His limbs were twisted. His feet were crooked. His body was distorted and deteriorated. The clock had struck three.

It was time for prayer. They could have gathered up their belongings, stepped up their pace and swept clean away from this miserable man, leaping up into the temple to pray. But Peter and John fastened their eyes. Fixed their gaze. Trained their attention on the man on the ground.

Something was about to happen because whenever the church looks in the power of the Holy Spirit at hurting people, something amazing is about to take place. A change is on the way. A new day is about to break.

Peter and John said to the poor man, "Look at us! Can't you see something different about us? Can't you see the beauty of God in us? Can't you see the joy of Jesus radiating from us? Can't you see the presence of the Holy Spirit in us? Look at *us*!

"Can't you see our eyes burning with the holy love of God? Can't you see that our hands are ready to do God's will? Look at our feet standing on the promises of Jesus. Look at our heads touched and anointed with Holy Spirit intelligence and baptized reason. Look at our faces shining luminously with the glory of the Lord Jesus. Look at *us*!

"We are somebody. We belong to somebody. We've been somewhere. We've received something. We've seen something. We've heard something. We know something. We've got something. Look at *us!*"

And my prayer for all of us who have shared this glorious time as part of the 20th Baptist World Congress is that as we leave this august gathering, we will be able to say with confidence to this doubtful world that if you want to view exhibit number one of what God and grace can do: look at us.

If you want to know that Jesus lives and Jesus saves, that Jesus can heal and bless and deliver: look at us. That the Spirit still speaks: look at us. If you don't believe that God will keep you all along this mortal way, that God will use you despite your human limitations, that God will open doors for you and hold them open until you get there, that God will make a way for you and deliver you from demons, death, destruction and trouble: look at us. Through many dangers, toils and snares, I have already come. It was grace that brought me safe thus far and grace will lead me on. That poor, paralyzed man looked at Peter and John expecting a great big donation. Most of the people who passed by just threw him a penny or two, but for once in his life, somebody looked at him and he looked back at these children of God and began to calculate in his head how much he would get. He wanted a handout.

Little did he realize that God was about to give him strength and ability to make his own way. God can do more than just give you a handout; God will give you a handup and that has to be the focus of our assistance around the globe.

God wants us to give more than just a check of charity; God wants us to empower people to stand on their own. God wants us to do more than give the hungry a fish sandwich; God wants us to provide some hooks and tackle and teach others how to fish for themselves.

The man expected a handout, but Peter gave him something else. It's there in verses 6-7: a donation, a stipulation and a transformation. Verse 6 declares, "Then Peter said, 'Silver and gold I do not have, but what I have

I give to you. In the Name of Jesus Christ of Nazareth: rise up and walk.'"
There's the donation.

All the man wanted was money, but he needed more than money. Money
helps, but money doesn't heal. Money can buy a house, but money can't
make a home. Money can buy cars and clothes, but money cannot buy
character and contentment. Money can purchase a higher standard of
living, but money cannot buy quality of life.

Peter and John said, "We don't have any money. We left all to follow Jesus.
We can't buy you bread. We can't pay your rent. We can't catch up your
bills, but we still have something and we'll give you what we have. I don't
have what you want, but I have what you need. I don't have money, but I
give you Jesus." That's the donation and I want to encourage you today to
give what you have.

Don't ever think that what you have does not matter. You don't have to
speak like Shakespeare in order to testify. You don't have to preach like
Paul before you can proclaim. You don't have to sing like angels before you
can offer your praise. You don't have to give millions before you can make
a difference.

If the church would be built, if families would be strengthened, if nations
would be transformed, if the kingdom would be advanced, if praises would
be sung, if sinners would be saved and if cripples would be healed: we must
use what we have. What you have is more important than what you don't
have. You can change the world with what you have. You can solve your
problems with what you have. You can rise above your hurts with what you
have. You can overcome with what you have.

You can get the victory with what you have. You can open any door,
remove any restriction, shatter any shackle, face any problem, speak in
any language, go anywhere, do anything and love anybody with what you
have. Peter said, "I don't have what you want, but I have something to give
you. I have a Christ that you don't know. I have the Holy Spirit you haven't
received. I have joy that you've never felt. I have a hope that will never

disappoint. I have a faith that will not shrink. A love that won't let you go. A fire that won't go out. A friend that won't forsake you. A God that won't leave you. A Christ that won't disappoint you. A life that won't end. Power you won't lose. Light that won't go out. In the Name of Jesus: get up and walk. That's the stipulation.

Make a move. The man said, "I can't do it. I've never stood. I'm not strong." Peter said, "Shut up, look up, get up and stand up and walk. Not in your name, not in your power, but in the Name of Jesus. In his name, you can do the impossible. In his name, your sins can be forgiven.

In his name, your life can be changed. In his name, your mountains can be moved. Your problems can be solved. Your burdens can be lifted. Your sickness can be healed. Your trouble can be conquered. Your heart can rejoice. Your feet can be straightened.

Jesus will fix it because he has the power, he is the power; he has the way, he is the way; he has the life, he is the life; he has the strength, he is the strength; he has the word, he is the word; he has the answer, he is the answer: in the name of Jesus – stand up.

The man had never considered walking as an option, but when he tried, he discovered a strength he had never known, energy he had never felt and a future he had never imagined. Peter stretched out his hand and helped him up on his feet and the higher he rose, the stronger he felt.

He came up a little higher and his bones snapped into joint. He came up a little higher and his limbs got straight. He came up a little higher and felt strength surge into his body. He pushed himself away from Peter. Took one great big leap. Landed flat on his own two feet, and said, "I feel something that I've never felt before. I believe that I can walk. Healing is here now. Deliverance is here now. Victory is here now." He lifted one foot and said, "Alleluia!" Lifted the other foot and said, "Bless His Holy Name." He went walking and leaping all over the place. Then he caught sight of Peter and John going in the church and said, "Wait for me. I want to go with you. I was glad when they said unto me; let us go into the house of the Lord."

He went into the temple, sat down in the back, tried to be dignified, tried to be cool and quiet, tried to hold his peace. But something started moving on the inside and he jumped straight up in the air and said, "I've got to tell somebody what Jesus did for me. He lifted up my head, stood me on my feet and changed my destiny."

Somebody in the crowd said, "Please sit down and shut up. Don't you know where you are? You're a participant in the 20th Baptist World Congress. We don't do that in here. We're at the Convention Center." But the man said, "I just can't help it. I heard the Spirit and it's like fire shut up in my bones. He gave me a story; I have to tell it. He gave me a song; I have to sing it. He gave me a trumpet; I have to blow it. He gave me the victory; I have to share it."

That's my testimony today. "Jesus is all the world to me, my life, my joy, my all. He is my strength from day to day, without him I would fall, when I am sad, to him I go. No other one can cheer me so. When I am sad, he makes me glad. He's my friend."[1] In his name, we can change the world. In his name, changes can be made, mountains can be moved and doors can be opened.

In his name, hear the Spirit and if there's a life, you can live it. If there's a job, you can do it. If there's a need, you can meet it. If there's a challenge, you can face it. If there's sickness, you can heal it. If there is injustice, you can change it.

If there's a class, you can teach it. If there's a book, you can write it. If there's a song, you can sing it. If there's a story, you can tell it. If there is hell, you can reverse it. When you hear the Spirit, you will praise God, you will thank God, you will work for God, and you will live for God. Hear the Spirit speak and follow where God leads.

---

[1] From the hymn, "Jesus is all the world to me" by Will Thompson, 1847-1909.

PART III

CONGRESS PROGRAM

12. Summary of Proceedings

Julie Justus

Introduction

The 20th Baptist World Congress was an unforgettable event bringing together Baptist Christians from around the world in Honolulu, Hawai`i, from July 28 to August 1, 2010. Admittedly, it is impossible to record all of the proceedings of such a significant, extraordinary occasion where participants were encouraged to "Hear the Spirit." Therefore, we offer only a brief and limited summary of the proceedings of the congress.

Daily

Each day of the congress had a similar flow, offering participants a unique opportunity to worship and enjoy fellowship with the diverse global Baptist family. In the daily schedule was a morning celebration, Bible study, international music fest, mission in action, Congress Unplugged, Hawai`ian Time, as well as the exhibits. Each day culminated with an outstanding evening celebration.

Morning Celebration

In the morning, participants gathered together to start the congress day with corporate worship. The morning sessions were marked by energetic music offerings from around the world and thoughtful and stimulating plenary Bible study speakers. The keynote speakers were Pablo Deiros (Argentina), Janet Clark (Canada), Allan Demond (Australia) and Lance Watson (USA). Daily scripture readers shared the word of God in their own heart language and ecumenical leaders, invited by the BWA, gave greetings from their world communions. The large group assembly also provided the opportunity for organizers to highlight the various aspects of BWA's ministry with adept informational video vignettes. The vivacious morning celebration was an encouragement for participants to "Hear the Spirit" as it set the tone for the rest of the day.

Bible Studies

After the morning celebration, congress participants broke into small Bible study groups to further discuss Luke 4:18-19, the congress, theme text: "The Spirit of the Lord is on me, because he has anointed me to proclaim good news to the poor. He has sent me to proclaim freedom for the prisoners and recovery of sight for the blind, to set the oppressed free, to proclaim the year of the Lord's favor." (*New International Version*)

In order to meet the language needs of the majority of congress participants, the Bible study groups were offered in Chinese, English, French, German, Japanese, Korean, Portuguese and Spanish.

Many gifted Baptists were approached to lead the multiple language Bible studies. The six English groups were facilitated by: Alistair Brown, Jonathan Edwards, William Epps, Randel Everett, Julie Pennington-Russell, Peter Pinder, Emile Sam-Peale and Rachael Tan. The other seven languages offered each had one group, respectively. The Bible study leaders were: Chinese – Meilin Chen and Wood-Ping Chu; French – Adebola Fatokun, Samson Fatokun, and Terry Smith; German – Regina Claas and Volkmar Hamp; Japanese – Shigemi Ono, Hikofumi Tomari and Makito Watanabe; Korean – Steve (Sekyu) Chang, John Jung Ryong, and Myung Jim (Joseph) Ko; Portuguese – Marlene Baltazar da Nóbrega Gomes and Fausto Vasconcelos; and Spanish – Daniel Carro, Raquel Contreras, and Alberto Prokopchuk.

The language Bible study groups offered a smaller, perhaps more intimate, way for congress attendees to "Hear the Spirit" as they discussed the Word of God in their heart language.

International Music Fest

While there were official meal "breaks" during the congress, the opportunity to be blessed by the global nature of the event continued during the lunch and dinner time slots through the International Music Fest.

The International Music Fest organizers invited congress participants to bring along food to the event where they could experience the abundant diversity Baptists have in worship and culture via religious and national music.

The individual and group artists, both amateur and professional, hailed from an assortment of countries including Brazil, Canada, Korea, Latvia, Nagaland (India), New Zealand, Norway, Trinidad and Tobago and the United States. Of special note were the several artistic contributions made by the Hawaiian hosts throughout the week.

The music shared at the International Music Fest blessed attendees as artists demonstrated their unique culture and perspective, indeed proving to be one of the memorable experiences at the congress.

Congress Unplugged

Congress Unplugged was yet another option for enrichment during the scheduled meal breaks. These informal sessions were designed to provide an opportunity for attendees to hear more from leaders of the Baptist movement and other congress presenters. For example, conversations were facilitated on topics such as the perspective of women leaders as advocates for the voiceless, the Baptist impact on church "leavers," how churches are reaching emerging generations, and international trends in Baptist life. These times of sharing provided another unique opportunity for participants to "Hear the Spirit" through the mutual respect of diverse opinions and experiences.

Mission in Action

In the afternoon, congress attendees were encouraged to participate in various Mission in Action projects. This endeavor originated from the commitment of congress organizers to make the meeting of Baptists meaningful and memorable for both the participants and the surrounding community in Honolulu and beyond.

These mission project opportunities took place both inside and outside the conference center. For example, the congress reached out to the homeless community by offering meals and hygiene kits. Moreover, participants helped to paint a shelter ministering to the local homeless population.

Stop Hunger Now, a group which, according to its website, "is an international hunger relief organization that coordinates the distribution of food and other life-saving aid around the world," partnered with the Baptist World Congress to assist volunteers in preparing 30,000 well-balanced meals to be distributed in Honolulu and beyond.

The Mission in Action projects enabled congress participants to use their hands to make a difference for Christ while expanding their understanding of fellowship and cooperation.

Hawaiian Time

The local Hawaiian hosts said "Aloha" to their guests by providing informative afternoon Hawaiian Time sessions. These seminars, led by Hawaiians, were advertised as "gatherings enabling you to learn about and experience the uniqueness of our Islands."

The four diverse and interactive seminars offered were: The Hula – Grace, Power and Beauty; God's Legacy in Hawai`i; The Gospel Comes to Hawai`i – the Early Years; and the Joy of the Ukulele. These sessions were a popular afternoon destination for many congress participants. Attendees of the Hula tutorial were even invited to dance with teacher Beth Lazor at the International Music Fest.

The Hawaiian time truly gave Baptists attending the congress an excellent glimpse into the distinct culture, tradition and history of the host islands.

Exhibits

Throughout the day, whenever congress participants found free time, those working in the Exhibit Hall were ready to share about their ministries. Twenty-eight organizations had booths, and in order to encourage attendees to visit all of the exhibits, a Circle the World Drawing was held on Saturday for all those who could present a completed card proving that they had indeed stopped by each ministry's booth.

Of the twenty-eight booths, the space dedicated to the BWA was certainly a highlight. The BWA booth, with a warm and welcoming environment, provided visitors with a deeper understanding of the global church body hosting the congress. Those who stopped by were able to view informative presentations of the general secretary and his travels, the history of the BWA, various areas of BWA's ministry, as well as the work in the various BWA regions, while listening to music from around the world. In addition, participants were offered BWA materials in nine different languages and given the opportunity to sign up to receive regular informational updates from the BWA Center. The BWA booth was also the home to videos of the fellowship occurring at the 2010 Congress.

Evening Celebration

The congress day culminated with an evening plenary celebration. These gatherings, much like the morning assemblies, enabled participants to engage in multicultural worship experiences. The congress hall was filled with the Spirit as ecumenical leaders gave greetings, the worship band played and the many choirs from around the world sang. Truly an international event, the plenary sessions, both morning and evening, had simultaneous translation for French, Japanese, Portuguese and Spanish speakers.

The evening celebration's main speakers: David Coffey (United Kingdom), Karl Johnson (Jamaica), Alongla Aier (Nagaland, India) and Ngwedia Paul Msiza (South Africa); brought their own unique perspective as they urged Baptists to renew their commitment to hearing God's Spirit.

Each evening, as the offering was taken to support the ministry of the Baptist World Alliance, Baptists responded by generously giving to the work of the movement. At the conclusion of the evening celebration service, the final benediction was given by a BWA leader who sent congress participants out until they gathered again the next morning to continue the incomparable Baptist World Congress experience.

Different Tracts

While the congress adult participants went about their day, there were also concurrent tracts for both the teens and the children attending the Baptist World Congress.

Youth Program

The Congress Youth tract was organized by Passport, a camp affiliated with the United States' Cooperative Baptist Fellowship which operates with the mission statement: "With Christ as our foundation, Passport empowers students to encounter Christ, embrace community, and extend grace to the world." The four Passport leaders recruited twelve volunteers from around the world to help facilitate the overall program for 120 youth participants from more than fifteen countries.

Each day, the youth had a time of worship, led by the Baptist Student Ministry from the University of Hawai'i. During the sessions, the director of the program, Virginian Greg Harrell, spoke on the importance of the youth being involved in discipleship and evangelism at home, based on the Romans 10:15 theme verse: "How beautiful are the feet of those who bring good news." After hearing the message, the youth were divided into small groups in order to foster a deeper level of sharing.

Other notable aspects of the youth program included both learning about and experiencing Hawaiian culture and history. This endeavor included time for instruction as well as field trips to the Ala Moana beach and the Diamond Head volcanic crater. The youth also took part in the congress Mission in Action projects by preparing 13,000 of the Stop Hunger Now meals that were packaged during the week.

All the youth who participated in the program benefited from the many fellowship, worship and multi-cultural age-appropriate opportunities provided at the congress.

Children's Program

The congress organizers made arrangements for a special tract for the children attending the event. Forty children from eight countries experienced their own part of the congress, led by Deborah Upton, an associate pastor from Virginia, USA.

With help from volunteers, Upton engaged the children, aged five to eleven, in various activities including arts and crafts, games and Bible stories. The children also joined the youth in their Mission in Action meal preparation project.

For the parents of children, as well as those attending the plenary session, the highlight of the children's program was to see the children on stage singing "He's Got the Whole World in his Hands" during the congress Saturday evening celebration. What a joy it was to see the diverse group of children wearing their own handmade leis, and singing about their unity in Christ. The congress heard the Spirit through their young and vivacious voices.

Special Events

While the congress did have a regular daily schedule, several special noteworthy events occurred throughout the conference.

Regional Meetings

Regional meetings were held on Thursday and Friday afternoons. With each of the six BWA regions having one session, the congress participants were able to gather with those from their own continental grouping in order to share, discuss and plan. The time to gather at a Baptist World Congress is an invaluable opportunity for each region of the BWA to meet together.

The BWA Regional Secretaries convened the following meetings:

Region	Regional Secretary
All Africa Baptist Fellowship	Harrison Olan'g
Asia Pacific Baptist Federation	Bonny Resu
Caribbean Baptist Fellowship	Peter Pinder
European Baptist Federation	Tony Peck
Union of Baptists in Latin America	Alberto Prokopchuk
North American Baptist Fellowship	George Bullard

Focus Groups

On Thursday and Friday, there were seventeen different focus groups designed for small group discussion on a multitude of theological, social and ethical topics. Congress organizers created the groups with the five BWA clusters of commitment in mind: worship and fellowship; mission and evangelism; religious liberty and human rights; relief and sustainable development; and relevant theological reflection. The many Focus Group presenters and facilitators hailed from around the world, thus offering a variety of perspectives and backgrounds.

Women's Rally

On Saturday afternoon, approximately 1,000 women attended the women's rally. The inspirational gathering included testimonies, videos and songs on the afternoon's theme, "In Step with the Spirit." Special emphasis was placed on the upcoming Baptist Women's World Day of Prayer in November 2010. The Women's Department's newly elected officers were presented at the rally: Raquel Contreras, president; Donna Groover, secretary/treasurer; and one new vice president from the Caribbean, Yvonne Pitter. The women left the meeting celebrating what God is doing in the lives of Baptist women around the world.

Men's Rally

Occurring concurrently with the women's rally, the men's rally brought together approximately 200 men. Forestal Lawton, outgoing Men's Department president; incoming Men's Department president, Owen Crooks; David Coffey, outgoing BWA president; and John Upton, incoming BWA president, all addressed the gathering. The meeting also provided an opportunity for the Men's Department to install new officers. Those installed during the meeting were: Owen Crooks (Jamaica), president; Doyle Pennington (USA), secretary; Harold Wolgast (USA), treasurer; and Forestal Lawton (USA), director. The Men's Department invited all those present at the rally to participate in their upcoming Men's World Day of Prayer in April 2011.

Living Water Celebration

After the rallies on Saturday afternoon, congress attendees were invited to help celebrate the ministry of Living Water, a special BWA evangelism emphasis under the leadership of Fausto Vasconcelos and Tony Cupit. In a worship service that featured many of the elements used in the Living Water conferences that had occurred around the world during the previous five years, this truly global event incorporated musical selections offered by artists of a variety of nationalities. Additionally, the worship service included testimonies and a drama presentation with an international cast. As the keynote speaker, BWA General Secretary Callam stressed the importance of BWA's ongoing commitment to evangelism and invited the gathering to support the Bread of Life thrust for the next five years of BWA's evangelism program. The culmination of the Living Water ministry at the congress well represented the formal conclusion of an outstanding evangelism prototype in the Baptist world.

Baptist 400 Fund

It is worth noting that throughout the week, participants were given the opportunity to contribute to the Baptist 400 Fund. Launched in 2009 following the 400th anniversary of the birth of the historic Baptist movement, the fund provides an avenue for Baptists to invest in the future of the BWA while celebrating our rich heritage. Prior to the congress, registrants were asked to bring a gift in the equivalent of 40, 400, 4,000 or 40,000 units of their local currency. More than 200 Baptists attending the congress contributed to the Baptist 400 Fund.

Conclusion

The program elements of the 20th Baptist World Congress give just a glimpse into the affairs of the meeting. What cannot be recorded, however, are the countless unprogrammed events, such as the conversations and lifelong friendships made by Baptists gathered at the event. While it is impossible to measure the impact on those attending and how individuals and groups were able to "Hear the Spirit" throughout the week, it can be said that a BWA Congress is truly a special and unmatchable event in the life of the worldwide Baptist family.

13. The Focus Groups

Neville Callam

The vision statement of the Baptist World Alliance (BWA) identifies the organization as "a global movement of Baptists sharing a common confession of faith in Jesus Christ bonded together by God's love to support, encourage and strengthen one another, while proclaiming and living the gospel of Jesus Christ in the power of the Holy Spirit before a lost and hurting world."

Arising from the work of its Twenty-First Century Committee which proposed this vision statement, the BWA adopted five "clusters of commitment" that point out the contours of the organization's priorities. These are worship and fellowship, mission and evangelism, religious liberty and human rights, relief and sustainable development, and relevant theological reflection. The first four clusters identify areas of concern and the last refers to the method to be employed in pursuit of ecclesial vocational integrity.

The committee appointed to develop the list of topics to be discussed in "focus groups" at the 20th Baptist World Congress had the BWA priorities before them as they set out to do their work. After this committee, chaired by David Goatley,[1] presented its proposal at the BWA Annual Gathering in Ede, the Netherlands, the focus group program for the Hawai`i congress was finalized.

The focus groups met in two two-hour sessions of the congress. Moderated by active participants in the ministry of the BWA, two presenters addressed each session after which those assembled engaged in discussion. In some cases, the same presenters served in the two sessions set aside for each focus group.

[1] For information on Focus Group moderators and presenters, see Appendix 3.

Worship and Fellowship

Four forums focused on issues related to worship and fellowship. The first, moderated by Tony Peck, considered "A Balm in Gilead: Worship that heals the broken." Presenters agreed that disciples of Jesus Christ encounter God through corporate worship. The question they sought to address was: "How do we worship God when our life experiences leave us hurt, wounded, and broken?" The presenters — Burchell Taylor, Samuel Otu Pimpong, and Joel Sierra — explored how worship can help to lead broken people and communities toward new horizons.

In the words of Taylor, worship is "God-initiated, God-focused and God-inspired." On account of this, in response to the invitation and promise of worship, Taylor explained how "the hard-pressed and truly shattered ... find healing in the disclosure and assurance that worship makes available."

The second forum under worship and fellowship dealt with "Embracing and Releasing: Do Christians ever need to abandon their cultures?" Understanding that Jesus calls his followers to love God with all their heart, soul, and strength, the presenters discussed how Jesus' disciples live in the tension of competing claims of the Gospel and their cultural customs and traditions. Gary Nelson moderated the group discussions where presenters, Graham Walker, Henry Mugabe, Solomon Ishola, and Wanne Garrey, examined how Christians living in challenging contexts may still live with integrity in the Spirit.

After exploring a paradigm for relating Christianity and culture, Solomon Ishola explained how, through a process of indigenization, contextualization, inculturation and incarnation, Christians have endeavored to relate the Gospel and culture. He called upon Christians to adopt "a life of integrity that requires faithfulness to biblical revelation and relevance to a particular receiving culture."

"Priscilla, Aquila, and Apollos: Effective mentoring for emerging leaders" was the topic of the third forum under worship and fellowship. Agreeing that all leaders need others to help them develop into stronger leaders, the presenters considered how, given the huge demands on current effective Christian leaders, they might effectively nurture new generations of leaders for the church.   The presenters – Chris Liebrum, Warren Stewart, Brian Winslade, and Denise de Vasconcelos Araujo – offered perspectives on contemporary models for mentoring emerging leaders locally and globally.

Presenters agreed on the wisdom and discernment needed for the multifaceted process of mentoring. As Brian Winslade put it, "Those who effectively and deliberately mentor emerging leaders give the church a great gift. They ensure its future and resource it with men and women capable of leading God's people to ever greater works of mission in God's world."

Fausto Vasconcelos, who moderated one of the sessions, reported that the main focus of the discussions was on succession in the pastorate, that is transition from one pastor to another. Ellen Teague, who moderated the other session, said the emphasis of her group was on the Emerging Leaders Network that had been formed in the BWA in the quinquennium that ended at the congress.

The fourth forum discussed the subject, "The Exhausted Leader: How do I lead when my faith is low?" The presenters – Wilbert Goatley, George Bullard and Mauricio Droguette – said that Christian leaders tend to give generously of themselves and to have people frequently drawing on, asking for, and taking from, them. In their presentations, they focused on the leaders' obligation to take care of themselves even while caring for others.

The presenters offered advice on how to avoid exhaustion. Urging Christian leaders to engage in, and profit from, self-care, George Bullard emphasized how active involvement in multiple relationships of accountability and getting back in touch with the rhythms of life are practices of leaders who have learned the secret of self-care. Lewis Petrie moderated the discussion on how vulnerable leaders become when faith is low.

Mission and Evangelism

Seven forums addressed issues related to mission and evangelism. The first of these, entitled, "Salt of the Earth: Faith, Life and Witness in multi-cultural contexts," considered how disciples of Jesus Christ, who are called "the salt of the earth," may have an impact on the world for God's glory and for humanity's good. The presenters – Tom Mei, Robert Cochran, Nabeeh Abbassi and Hanho Doh – considered how Christians can be authentic witnesses to Jesus Christ in communities and countries where different beliefs, practices, and truth claims compete for the hearts and minds of people.

Mei proposed two key strategies Christians need to employ in the search for effective ways to let their light shine where multiple faiths exist. First, they are to value mutually transformational partnerships. Second, they are to intentionally pay attention to what God is doing and then find ways to be involved. The forum was moderated by Jonathan Edwards.

"Baptists at 400: Where have we been and where should we go?" was the theme of the second focus group under the rubric of mission and evangelism. "Devon Dick, Karen Bullock, Daniel Carro and Blake Killingsworth made presentations at the sessions chaired by Cawley Bolt. They each probed the trajectories of Baptist life and witness and attempted to forecast where Baptist expressions might be headed in the twenty-first century.

Describing the Baptist story as "the result of God's calling, gifts, and empowering," Bullock said Baptists have been supported by God's sustaining grace. "With great sensitivity," she added, "Baptists also need to face global challenges in the days ahead, including identity and doctrinal variations across our varied expressions of family life, how positive dialogue and biblical unity may be best expressed among peoples of other faith communions and world religions, and the dire necessity for holistic, transformational justice ministries within our local communities, states, and nations."

Another forum considered the topic, "Serving the Present Age: Exploring entrepreneurial missional models." Chaired by David Goatley, the forum investigated relevant and interesting ways in which disciples are responding to the call to be the church today.

The presenters, Peter Mihaere, John Beasy and Michael Stroope, showed how, in each generation, the church seeks to live out its calling as the body of Christ. They identified ways in which the multiple changes in the world require the church to take innovative approaches to ministry. In the words of Stroope, "To discover new ways of service and witness requires that we dive headlong into the convergence, the mixture where gospel and context meet. Such bold, and yet humble, innovation produces faithful service in the present age, to every locale."

In another forum, participants discussed the subject, "Immersion or Tourism: The ethics of short-term mission trips." They noted that many Christians are able to travel for worship, service and conferences to places that others visit merely for pleasure. Robert Nash, Olu Menjay, James Hill and Brenda Harewood suggested ways in which Christians may experience "exotic" places in the world without exploitation. Moderator, Jerry Carlisle, led the group in a discussion on how Christian disciples can make a lasting and loving impact in tourism centers around the world.

According to Carlisle, the presentations included "a historical perspective on the current phenomenon of short-term trips under the title of 'mission,' as well as a discussion of the various degrees of effectiveness of the increased number of such trips." The potential for these short-term trips to be beneficial was explained in terms of the opportunity for "gateway experiences for those whom God will call to more substantial involvement, initiating partnerships that can be developed for longer-term ministry, occasionally actually accomplishing work of spiritual significance, and opening funding doors for future collaboration." Meanwhile, the problematic areas identified include "financial disparity which can be demeaning to those 'receiving' ministry; cultural insensitivity which can render an expensive effort not only futile, but damaging to ongoing work; ethical concern regarding the expense of sending 'tourists' compared to the benefit of simply sending the amount of money that would be spent on travel to those in the field for their continuing work." Despite these, the focus group members generally agreed that "short-term mission trips where senders and receivers intentionally share strategy and spiritual sensitivity can be a wonderful beginning point for ongoing ministry and continued relationships," Carlisle said.

"Crises in Church Leadership: What happens if family members do not believe?" was the focus of the fifth forum under mission and evangelism. Based on the suggestion that many people expect church leaders to enjoy and to exhibit exemplary models of personal and family life, the presenters considered how church leaders and the communities they serve respond to crises of faith in the leaders' homes.

Moderated by Regina Claas, the group listened to papers by Karen Kirlew, James Jackson and John Kok. Through case studies, analysis of the stages of psychosocial development, and reflection on personal encounters, presenters focused on the challenges involved when some in a church leader's family do not believe in Jesus.

In the fifth group dealing with the mission of the church, the theme was, "Pastoral Leadership amidst change: How churches minister to unmarried couples." Presentations were made by by Kwame Adzam, Johnathan Hemmings and William Wilson. They agreed that, in many parts of the world, ways of understanding the family and the household are changing. Reflecting on ministry approaches in contexts where unmarried people share households and raise children, the presenters suggested ways in which the church may minister among couples who are not married.

According to moderator, David Kerrigan, the presentations reflected the reality of a growing number of couples living together before marriage and revealed that "though more prevalent in westernized societies, there is a global trend emerging, driven by both economic and cultural pressures." Adding that the group considered how the church can best respond to this phenomenon, Kerrigan noted that the "emphasis was on how to simultaneously uphold biblical ideals and yet encourage cohabiting couples to find a welcome in our churches." He added that the group shared the view that "trial 'cohabitation' does not increase the chances of lasting relationships; in fact quite the contrary. But we recognized also what is called the 'trajectory of grace' – a cohabiting couple drawing closer to the church might be handled in a way different to, say, two Christian youth leaders who decided to live together. An 'intentional inconsistency' is justified because of the different trajectories." Reflecting on the focus group experience, Kerrigan noted that "in a forum comprising many nationalities and cultures, there was significant agreement on a compassionate response to those whose lifestyle choices have been formed without the experience of biblical teaching."

Another focus group worked with the theme: "Christian and Muslim Siblings: Children of Abraham and Sarah and Hagar." The forum participants acknowledged that different views exist concerning what contributes to contemporary tension between some expressions of both Christianity and Islam. Recognizing that Jews, Christians, and Muslims share a common heritage of the Abrahamic tradition, presenters – Nabil Costa, Johnson Lim, Robert Sellers, and Harrison Olan'g – sought to imagine a future of peaceful coexistence and the possibility of collaboration among larger parts of Christian and Muslim communities.

Moderator Roy Medley reported that "presenters sought to address a number of issues: historical causes for the conflict between Muslims and Christians; reflections upon the current state of relationships between Christians and Muslims from African, Asian, Middle Eastern and North American perspectives; and practical steps that might be taken toward developing positive relationships between the two faiths." He noted that "the issues that dominated the conversation following the presentations revolved around the subject of fundamentalist Islam." According to Medley, "The richness of the presentations lay in part in the diversity of regional perspectives. The face of Islam and of Christianity and their interrelationship varies in each setting. The presenters, speaking from their contexts, threw light on the complexity of the relationship depending upon one's locale."

Religious Liberty and Human Rights

Four focus groups discussed urgent issues of justice and human rights. The first, which was based on the theme, "Setting Captives Free: Anti-trafficking ministry and advocacy," described human trafficking as a devastating, yet lucrative, business. The group discussed how the church is to minister to those who are victimized by the dehumanizing practice of trafficking as a form of contemporary slavery. The presenters, Suzii Paynter, Zhanuo Sanchu and Vladimir Ubeivolc, examined ways of advocacy and action, and models of prophetic and compassionate ministry.

Focus group moderator, Lauran Bethell, reported that the presenters as "practitioners from different parts of the world with specific experience with the issue of human trafficking ... shared their call and passion for working against human trafficking. They also described how Baptists and other Christians in their context are involved... The presentations were practical in nature. They dealt with what people are doing to intervene with prevention, after-care, and political action." In the discussion that followed, according to Bethell, "people wanted to know what they could do about human trafficking in their context. They wanted to know how they could become involved ... An important outcome is that we decided we needed a Baptist database of anti-trafficking ministries around the world. Regularly updated documentation of this kind would provide people with information that persons could use to become involved." According to Bethell, the kind of networking and information sharing that the focus group afforded was invaluable. She suggested that, in the future, it would be beneficial to gather the practitioners for mutual support and encouragement.

The second focus group under freedom and justice discussed the subject, "Costly Christian Witness: The persecution of Christians in the twenty-first century." Noting that many Christians have suffered persecution because of their commitment to Jesus Christ, the group discussed contemporary experiences of persecution and ways in which the church may work on behalf of those who suffer for the Gospel. Elijah Brown, Christer Daelander and Blooming Night Zan made presentations in sessions moderated by Jeremy Bell.

Case studies were presented from different contexts – Sudan, Azerbaijan, Serbia, Belarus, Moldova, Turkmenistan, Macedonia, Italy, and the Karen people on the border of Thailand and Myanmar. As Elijah Brown observed, the church has a compelling obligation to garner "insights ... about strategies and tools that are effective in engaging areas of religious marginalization and injustice."

Participants in another focus group examined the subject, "Domination over every living thing? Christian discipleship and the environment." Given the conviction that the physical environment is undergoing degradation, the presenters – Michael Taylor, Bonny Resu, Helle Liht and Johnny Hill – considered how disciples of Jesus Christ might respond reasonably and caringly to the groaning of creation.

According to moderator, Ross Clifford, the main thrust of the presentations was that "Christians have a biblical responsibility as stewards to care for the environment and all of creation (Genesis 1 & 2) and that creation groans in expectation of being set free from the bondage of decay (Cf. Romans 8:21,22)." Clifford noted that the discussion following the presentation centered on how individuals, churches and the Baptist World Alliance can live out the mandate of creation care and educate the Christian and world community. As Johnny Hill explained, because the poor need to have adequate food and clean water, "the ways in which Christians ... think about ecological issues must be grounded in the persistent quest for justice, which includes not only fair and equitable distribution of the earth's resources but access to modern medicine, shelter, education, and a world free of violence and domination as well."

In the focus group which discussed the topic, "Everything God Made Was Very Good: The ethics of genetic engineering," presenters noted that scientific advances now make it possible to significantly alter the genetic makeup of all that lives. How might Christians engage theologically with the technological advances that enable people to re-engineer life?

Clayton Teague and Bill Tillman explored Christian perspectives on altering parts of God's creation. According to moderator, Raimundo Barreto,

Teague's scientific presentation traced the development of the process and described the great promise that technological developments hold. He also identified some of the risks involved, such as bioterrorism and eugenics.

Tillman provided a Christian ethical approach that dismissed the ethics of either/or, based on dichotomy and dilemmas, as insufficient and inappropriate to deal with the challenges posed by the new developments. He proposed an approach that bridges the artificial science-religion abyss, and provides a praxis that is relational, apologetic, and watchful. Both Teague and Tillman affirmed a positive link between the good of God's creation and the continuity of that creation through the creativity God has given to humankind.

The fourth focus group under Freedom and Justice discussed, "Stewardship and Hospitality: The ethics of tourism." Presentations were made by Deonie Duncan and Rod Benson in sessions moderated by Emmanuel McCall. There was general agreement on the important contribution tourism makes to the economy of many nations, but concerns were expressed about the tourism's effect on a country's development. This focus group explored the relation of tourism and environmental degradation, fair employment practices, and the preservation of host cultures.

Drawing upon the findings of a case study conducted in her country, Duncan identified unfair employment practices and danger to the preservation of the values in host cultures as two of the major ethical challenges of tourism. Over against these, she asserted human dignity, culture as a divine gift, and creation care as values that may be called into service to counteract negative consequences of tourism.

After describing the features of the Global Code of Ethics of the World Tourism Organization, Rod Benson explained that the call to Christian discipleship requires us to allow "our deepest Christian values and commitments ... to permeate every aspect of political, economic and social life" including modern service industries.

Relief and Development

The sole focus group addressing specifically the issue of relief and development used the title, "Best Practices Workshop in Relief and Development: Project design, proposal development, and project monitoring and evaluation." This workshop was designed for leaders in aid and development ministries among the member bodies of the Baptist World Alliance. The aim was to offer an opportunity for training in procedures for relief and response in situations of natural disasters. The workshop also provided insights into community development models and successes. The presenters – Kabi Gangmei, Terry Hamrick, Les Fussell and Bela Szilagyi – spoke against the background of years of experience in different parts of the world.

Theological Reflection

The planners of the focus groups expected that the discussion of the matters under consideration would be marked by responsible theological reflection. Congress participants attending the focus groups expected to be led in grappling seriously with the issues raised in the light of what they believe about God and God's will for human life. Together with the use of reason, discussants drew upon the font of their experience and the storehouse of divine revelation in the process of discerning a responsible Christian response to the issues.

Participants welcomed the range of issues dealt with by the congress focus groups. They praised the quality of the presentations and discussions in the groups. They also suggested that the focus groups represented a beneficial way for Baptists to spend time together at a meeting that is held once in each five-year period.

Neville Callam
General Secretary
Baptist World Alliance

14. From Birmingham to Honolulu and Beyond:

Moving in Step with the Holy Spirit

BWA General Secretary's Congress Address

"What has brought the delegates to Philadelphia from all the ends of the earth?" That's the question Rev. P. T. Thomson raised in his address before the second Baptist World Congress in 1911. He continued: "A common name? No. A common cause? No. It is a common Lord... Who can draw [people] so diverse into the fellowship of this memorable week? Is there anyone else but He who by drawing us to Himself can draw us close to one another?"[1] With 7,000 Baptists from 30 countries gathered in Philadelphia, Thomson claimed that Baptist voices were "belting the whole wide world with a cordon of praise."[2]

Today, ninety-nine years later, based on the work of noted expert, Professor David Barrett, Baptists number more than 105 million! At this 20th Baptist World Congress, thousands of delegates have come from 105 countries. And we have assembled because we believe that, in the providence of God, we belong together. We desire to hear what the Spirit is saying today in order that we will be able to keep in step with the Holy Spirit.

---

[1] *The Baptist World Alliance, Second Congress, Philadelphia, June 19-25, 1911: Record of Proceedings*, Philadelphia: Harper & Brother Company, 1911, p. 399.
[2] *Ibid.*, p. 398.

When last we met in Birmingham, in our centenary year, we recalled, with great thanksgiving, the inauguration of the Baptist World Alliance. We celebrated the faithfulness of the God who is the same, yesterday, today and forever and we decided to fix our eyes firmly on Jesus Christ, the Living Water. We also pondered the way ahead as the global Baptist fellowship forged its way into its second century.

Since Birmingham, we have marked the 400th anniversary of the Baptist movement and, once again, notes of praise and thanks ascended to God. What a wonderful road we have traveled! And what marvelous opportunities we see as we focus on the journey ahead!

Today, the Baptist World Alliance, this vehicle for the expression of the essential oneness of Baptists worldwide, is a community of some 160,000 churches in 120 countries with more than 38 million baptized members. Ours is the calling to make room for other Baptists to participate in the unity of Baptists worldwide. During the quinquennium that is ending here in Hawai`i, BWA membership grew with the addition of four member bodies and with overall church membership increase of some three million. Meanwhile, we are in the process of finalizing applications from seven potential member bodies on four continents. Our goal must be nothing less than universal Baptist membership in the BWA.

It has been my joyful privilege, over the last three years, to meet and have fellowship with Baptists in the six regions of the BWA. Thanks be to God for the many believers who can gather for worship and fellowship on a weekly basis without let or hindrance. The nurture they receive is equipping them for the ministry of reconciliation.

We bless God for the work being done in the areas of mission and evangelism, in formation in faith and Christian discipleship, in the promotion and defense of freedom and justice for the vulnerable and those who are persecuted on account of their faith, and in service to the oppressed and all who suffer. We go forward still declaring with all of God's people: "one

Lord, one faith, one baptism" (Ephesians 4:5) and reflecting an unshakeable commitment to the Triune God. Only so will we move in step with the Holy Spirit.

Over the last five years, the BWA has completed the process of clarifying our current understanding of the purpose our worldwide movement has been assigned. Now, together we can say:

The Baptist World Alliance is a global movement of Baptists sharing a common confession of faith in Jesus Christ, bonded together by God's love to support, encourage and strengthen one another, while proclaiming and living the Gospel of Jesus Christ in the power of the Holy Spirit before a lost and hurting world.

During the quinquennium that is coming to an end, the BWA has sought renewal in its understanding of its God-given mission. We now craft our mission in terms of worship and fellowship, mission and evangelism, religious liberty and human rights, relief and development, and relevant theological reflection.

We rejoice that, at long last, we have initiated, within the structures of the BWA, a ministry department dedicated to dealing with issues of freedom and justice. With personnel secured for the purpose, we now expect to focus our efforts more intentionally in this area.

The journey continues and we are here in Hawai`i to hear what the Spirit has to say as we prepare to go forward.

Will it be an easy road? No! Not with many parts of the world being firmly held in the clutches of post-modernity without negotiating it well. Even within some parts of the Christian community, the authority of Jesus is being dishonored. Among too many, the Bible is undervalued, and some of the values that have served us well over the years are being vilified. Meanwhile, many people who are searching for meaning and purpose in life are left confused by the rampant revisionism crippling the witness of some churches. More light and truth will come from the Word of God, but the God who speaks is unchanging. More ways may be found to spread the Gospel, but the Gospel remains the same. "I am not ashamed of the Gospel, for it is the power of God to the salvation of all who believe" (Romans 1:16). Let this be our testimony.

The road ahead is wide open. It will not be an easy road! Not with the rate of poverty being what it is! Every single day, some 16,000 children die from hunger-related causes – one child every five seconds.

The world is dealing with its greatest financial and economic challenge since World War II. The financial turmoil that began in 2007 erupted into a full-blown economic crisis in September 2008, spawned rising unemployment, and now threatens to become a major humanitarian problem. Virtually no country has escaped the impact of the widening crisis, the effects of which are likely to be felt through 2011.[3]

It is estimated that the spike in global food prices in 2008, followed by the global economic recession in 2009 and 2010, pushed between 100 and 150 million people into poverty. The number of chronically hungry people has climbed to more than one billion, reversing gains in fighting malnutrition between 2000 and 2005.

The road ahead beckons us. It will not be an easy road. Not with injustice being so rampant around the world. Our world is brutalized by the crime of human trafficking. We are still held captive by an oppressive attitude toward women and children. We are saddled by the monster of ethnic conflict. We are still stained by the sin of racism. Even now, at the end of a decade that Baptists dedicated to the fight against racism, that cruel monster is still alive and well. Come, Holy Spirit, slay that dragon and set us free.

And today, we are still failing to respect the integrity of creation. Too often, our stewardship does not reflect the knowledge we have of God's love for all humankind and for all of creation.

---

[3] See World Bank Annual Report at http://siteresources.worldbank.org/ EXTAR2009/Resources/6223977-1252950831873/AR09_Complete.pdf accessed on May 20, 2010.

The road that lies before us is not an easy road. Not with millions living without the saving knowledge of Jesus Christ! The need is desperate. The task is daunting! "How shall they hear without a preacher?" But thanks be to God, "Everyone who calls upon the name of the Lord will be saved!"

Time rolls on and during the quinquennium that begins at the end of this congress, shall we not focus our attention on moving in step with the Holy Spirit? We go forward mindful of the fact that we are not unaided. We are a listening people, prepared to hear what the Holy Spirit is saying and ready to be obedient. In the power of the Holy Spirit, we will lead many out of darkness into God's marvelous light; we will help form many in the image of Christ; and we will render service to many who need to see the face of Jesus.

As we go forward, let this be our watchword: to stay in step with the Spirit, to walk in holiness and righteousness, to manifest the love and the grace of God, to proclaim the Gospel in word and deed, to present the face of Jesus in a world where wretchedness stamps its ugly face across the nations.

In the light of the promises of God, the future of worldwide Baptist witness is rich with possibilities. Let us courageously seize the opportunities our Lord provides to be even more faithful witnesses. Let us not turn aside from keeping in step with the Holy Spirit.

I end this presentation with a thought clothed in the slightly altered words of John Clifford who, as president, addressed the second BWA Congress in Philadelphia in 1911 – the congress to which we referred at the start of this presentation:

Brothers and sisters in Christ, rise up with courageous faith. Convert your convictions into deeds. Gather determination to keep in step with the Holy Spirit until the earth is filled with the knowledge of the glory of God as the waters cover the sea.[4]

---

[4] Cf. The Baptist World Alliance, Second Congress, Philadelphia, June 19-25, 1911: Record of Proceedings, Philadelphia: Harper & Brother Company, 1911, p. 70.

15. From "Living Water" to "Bread of Life"

Living Water Celebration

Neville Callam

Evangelism needs a friend and that friend is servant leadership. Evangelism has a friend and that friend is servant leadership.

How indebted we are to our gracious God who has so wonderfully blessed the initiatives associated with the Living Water Strategy which we have pursued since 2005! Thousands of Baptist leaders and workers have been reminded of the priority of evangelism, of the compelling urgency of the commission to take the Gospel to the nations, telling all the people of the wonderful works of the one who calls us out of darkness into God's marvelous light.

The calling is unchanging; the calling to evangelize is as urgent now as it ever was. Many still need to know the transformation that God makes possible in Christ through the power of the Holy Spirit. They cannot be left to die in bondage to sin; we cannot close our eyes to their eternal destiny. Love impels us to bear witness to them in the name of Christ. Our Christian calling requires us to let them know the Good News of the one who offers the gift of salvation to everyone whom the Spirit leads to faith.

We will not shrink from our solemn obligation. We will, in word and deed, allow the Holy Spirit to illumine us so we can shed the light of truth in the darkness of the age and lead sinners to the one who enlightens and sets people free!

During the quinquennium that is coming to an end, we have sought to show the link between our evangelistic vocation and the calling to model the gift of servant leadership. We thank God for the many who have borne witness to this important Christian value and for the many who seek to live in its light.

We are on the cusp of a new quinquennium and now we are announcing that evangelism needs a friend and that friend is mission. We are affirming that evangelism has a friend and that friend is mission.

So here is a challenge for us today: Those who by God's grace are evangelized and continue to be evangelized need to become active participants in healthy churches – churches that understand the breadth of the engagement from which they cannot turn aside – as they commit themselves to the mission of the triune God through the church to the world.

We cannot weaken the bond of our unity in the evangelistic calling of the church; we cannot slacken the pace with which we commit to spread the Gospel of our Lord and Savior Jesus Christ. Nor can we abandon the complementary tasks that, together with direct evangelism, point out the contours of the vocation of the church.

In the new quinquennium, we will seek through our Bread of Life strategy to underline the link between evangelism and mission.

We live in an age when, if they are to believe, people need both to hear the message and to see it enacted. We must continue to offer a clear articulation of the Gospel that leads people to repentance and the gift of salvation. In this process, we must be intentionally incarnational. We must prophetically engage in the struggle against the powers of this world and manifest this in the witness we bear to the hungry and the lonely, to the sick and the imprisoned, to the stranger and the refugee, to those who are disturbed in spirit and to those who are caught up in the confusion of this age. In proclaiming the Gospel, we must rise to the challenge to respect the natural environment that God made, to respect the integrity of the creation that God loves. Evangelism with social witness is a compelling charge to the church.

This commitment is clearly stated in the Lausanne Covenant of 1974 which defines evangelism as "the proclamation of the historical, biblical Christ as Saviour and Lord, with a view to persuading people to come to him personally and so be reconciled to God ... The message of salvation implies also a message of judgment upon every form of alienation, oppression and discrimination ... When people receive Christ they are born again into [Christ's] kingdom and must seek not only to exhibit but also to spread its righteousness in the midst of an unrighteous world. The salvation we claim should be transforming us in the totality of our personal and social responsibilities."

Are you ready to affirm the bold thrust that will characterize the new phase of our unchanging commitment to evangelism: to affirm the friendship of evangelistic engagement and prophetic social action?

We will feed the poor, we will heal the sick and we will tell the world and show the people the wonders of the grace of our Lord Jesus Christ, the love of God and the fellowship of the Holy Spirit. But we will also prophetically critique those powers and structures that keep people from experiencing life in its fullness.

Are you ready to carry out the Great Commission so that the Bread of Life may nourish and enrich the nations? Are you ready to proclaim the Bread of Life so that the earth may be filled with the glory of God as the waters cover the sea?

Will you join us in this undertaking? God still asks, "Whom shall I send? And who will go for us?" May our answer always be, "Here am I. Send me!" Amen.

PART IV

CONGRESS INFORMATION

16. Congress Registrations by Country

Country	Total
Angola	58
Argentina	10
Australia	108
Austria	7
Bahamas	42
Bahrain	1
Bangladesh	107
Barbados	3
Bhutan	3
Bolivia	2
Brazil	212
Bulgaria	4
Burundi	4
Cambodia	2
Cameroon	8
Canada	108
Central African Republic	4
Chad	1
Chile	11
China	3
Colombia	2
Congo	6

Congo, The Democratic Republic of	165
Costa Rica	1
Cuba	3
Czech Republic	1
Denmark	10
Dominican Republic	2
Ecuador	5
El Salvador	1
Estonia	2
Fiji	9
Finland	7
France	1
Germany	21
Ghana	45
Grenada	3
Guyana	2
Haiti	18
Hong Kong	12
Hungary	6
India	278
Indonesia	5
Italy	1
Jamaica	130
Japan	76
Jordan	3
Kenya	30
Korea, Republic of	17
Latvia	1
Lebanon	6
Liberia	25
Macedonia	1
Malawi	5

Malaysia	23
Mexico	1
Moldova, Republic of	1
Myanmar	165
Namibia	2
Nepal	5
Netherlands	7
New Zealand	9
Nicaragua	1
Niger	1
Nigeria	275
Norway	120
Pakistan	6
Panama	1
Papua New Guinea	3
Paraguay	1
Peru	2
Philippines	11
Poland	1
Portugal	2
Puerto Rico	2
Qatar	1
Romania	3
Russian Federation	4
Rwanda	2
Serbia	3
Sierra Leone	32
Singapore	3
Slovakia	1
South Africa	15
Spain	2

Sri Lanka	3
Swaziland	1
Sweden	15
Switzerland	4
Taiwan	2
Tanzania, United Republic	4
Thailand	19
Togo	2
Trinidad and Tobago	23
Turkey	2
Turks and Caicos Islands	7
Uganda	10
Ukraine	6
United Kingdom	122
United States	1676
Venezuela	2
Vietnam	4
Western Sahara	1
Zambia	2
Zimbabwe	16
SUB-TOTAL Registrations	**4224**
Registrations on site	173
Day passes	935
TOTAL Registrations	**5332**
TOTAL Countries	**105**

17. Congress Program Committee

John Upton, Chair
Warren Stewart, Vice Chair
Kojo Amo
James Baucom
Jeremy Bell
Ronald Bobo
Alistair Brown
Carol Causey
Wood-Ping Chu
Regina Claas
Raquel Contreras
David Goatley
Solomon Ishola
Karl Johnson
Charles Jones
Jerry Jones
Joseph Kim
Victor Kulbich
Rick Lazor
Chris Liebrum
David Loder
Tomas Mackey
Janice Dando

William Epps
Dean Miller
Peter Mitskevich
Bob Morrison
Paul Msiza
Carla Nelson
Eli Fernandez de Oliveira
Teodor Oprenov
Eiji Osato
Jorge Pastor
Indranie Premawardhana
Jan Saethre
Emile Sam-Peal
Colin Saunders
Dorothy Selebano
Joel Sierra
Tom Song
Jenny Stewart
Bathsheba Stewart
William Thompson
Naomi Tyler-Lloyd
Charles Wade
Fermin Whittaker

18. Local Arrangements Committee

Rick Lazor, Chair
Walter Agena
Deanna Aoki
Liana Benn
Dwight Cook
Sharon Dumas
Lance Fairly
Veryl Henderson
Keri Kaneshiro
Andrew Large
Carlye Lawrence
Robert Miller
Nichole Nakamichi
Ken Suesz
Charlene Vaughn
John Vaughn
Makito Watanabe
Shirley Yuen

PART V

BWA INFORMATION

19. REPORT ON BWA MINISTRY, 2005-2010

During the 2005-2010 quinquennium, the divisions of the BWA have sought to carry out their mandate in the spirit of glad service to the Head of the Church and in the interest of the mission of the BWA. We are pleased to report on the work coordinated by the divisions.

What a wonderful privilege it is to have the opportunity to share in both the structured and spontaneous fellowship opportunities offered at the meetings of the BWA and its ministry teams! Who can forget the memorable experiences gained at the Centenary Congress in England? Since then, our Annual Gatherings in Mexico (2006), Ghana (2007), the Czech Republic (2008) and the Netherlands (2009), where we celebrated the 400th anniversary of continuous Baptist ministry, have allowed friendships to develop and new networking possibilities to see the light of day.

Among the youth, men and women, good use was made of fellowship opportunities where collaboration in mission was also evident.

Youth in Ministry

Even though the quinquennium presented unique challenges, the Youth Department was relentless in pursuing its strategic ministry priorities namely: Annual Youth World Day of Prayer, Leadership Development, Mission Awareness, and the Baptist Youth World Conference. These projects were sponsored in the service of supporting, strengthening and encouraging young people in Christian devotion and service.

The following is a synopsis of the work that has been undertaken for the period March 2005 – March 2010.

The second Sunday in June is celebrated each year as Baptist Youth World Day of Prayer. The day's program is designed for young people to reflect on the needs and challenges of others and to offer intercessions on their behalf. This celebration is also intended to offer opportunity for Baptist young people to contribute financially to the ministry of the Youth Department. Funds raised are deposited into a youth endowment account with interest going toward the funding of leadership training conferences. Approximately $20,000 was raised during this quinquennium and eight leadership training conferences were held.

Each year we make web-based material available to all for use on the Youth Day of Prayer. These materials include Bible studies, worship service outlines, readings on prayer, and prayer requests from around the world.

Eight leadership training conferences were held in the following countries: Ghana, Sierra Leone, Nigeria, Liberia, Hong Kong, Bolivia, Cameroon, and Germany. In addition, the BWA Youth Department helped coordinate, and participated in, conferences in the following countries: Lebanon, Cambodia, Trinidad, Bahamas, Argentina, Chile, India, Turkey, and the USA. We also provided financial assistance to the European Baptist Federation Youth Leadership training project, HORIZON, to assist with translating the training material into other languages to benefit those who cannot read English.

Beginning in 2009, we initiated an annual leadership training session for members of the Youth Executive and International Program Committees. The goal is to expose the members to new trends in youth ministries, strengthen their social networking skills, help them understand the unique challenges confronting young people, and assist them in developing a healthy appreciation for the gifts and skills that each brings to the global family.

More and more young people are being encouraged to engage in Christian mission. Young people are showing motivation to respond to the call to go into all the world. They are getting connected to other young people in meaningful ways. Undertaking mission projects together, youth are interacting with different cultures, leading to a deeper understanding and appreciation of one another. When such opportunities are provided through the BWA, they help our young people to develop a sense of belonging to the worldwide Baptist family.

It is with this in view, and in keeping with our objectives, that over the last five years, the Youth Department, in collaboration with other Baptist entities, facilitated and participated in mission projects in the following countries: Germany (in conjunction with the 2008 Baptist Youth World Conference in Leipzig), the Czech Republic, Austria, Italy, Egypt (in association with ABC USA) and Ghana.

In partnership with the Cambodia Baptist Union, we continue to support the Khmer Baptist House Project. This project provides housing for young boys coming from the villages and attending schools in the city. We committed a total of $6,000.00 over a three year period beginning in 2008. This partnership will conclude in December of 2010.

In collaboration with the All Africa Baptist Youth Fellowship and the BWA Living Water Initiative, 152 young people from seven African countries met in Ibadan, Nigeria, for a conference on youth evangelism. This was the first Living Water Conference planned solely for young people. Public evangelism rallies were held each evening and many first time decisions were made.

The 15th Baptist Youth World Conference, held in Leipzig, Germany, July 30 – August 3, 2008, and hosted by the German Baptist union, was a blessing to the 6,300 young people from ninety-seven countries who participated. Sponsored by the BWA, this once in every five year gathering of Baptist youth is designed to promote the cause of Christ and his church, facilitate interaction through cultural interchange, and engagement in mission projects. The training opportunities it provides helps equip young people for Christian service and fosters fellowship and good human relations.

Using the theme "Dive Deeper," the five day event was marked by daily morning worship and Bible study, afternoon discussion groups and training sessions, evening worship celebration services and an open air festival in the city center of Leipzig.

The Spirit moved in many ways and especially in the decisions that were made. Decision-makers were counseled by our care givers and information was passed on to their spiritual leaders.

Women in Ministry

Over the past five years, the BWA Women's Department has seen with new eyes Baptist women standing together, growing in effectiveness, and impacting our world for Christ. Dorothy Selebano, president from 2005-2010, led the BWA Women's Department Executive Board in the fulfillment of its mission to encourage and celebrate unity in Christ among Baptist women of the world and to work toward peace, reconciliation, justice and development through prayer, witness and service.

The elected officers, executive director and seven vice presidents form the BWA Women's Department Executive Board. This report reflects the work of this Board based on the four strategic priorities of the BWA Women's Department.

Women's development is an area of the BWA Women's Department ministry devoted to helping women grow to their full potential in order to impact the world around them. The following are achievements in this area.

Permission was granted to translate Joyce Cope Wyatt's book, *Soy Mujer! Soy Especial*! The English title is *I am a woman, Created in the Image of God*. The book was available at the Women's Leadership Conference and Baptist World Congress in Honolulu, Hawai`i.

The Baptist Women's Day of Prayer is at the core of the BWA Women's Department program. This annual observance on the first Monday of

November each year is the means for carrying out the mission of the organization. The five year theme has been "Seeing with New Eyes: God's Mercy, God's Compassion, God's Care, and God's Creation." Five different continental unions prepared the programs.

In 2005, at the Baptist Women's Leadership Conference in Birmingham, England, new continental union prayer partners were assigned as follows: BWUA-UFBAL; ABWU-NABWU; CBWU-NABWU; and EBWU-BWUSWP. During this quinquennium the different continental unions have encouraged prayer as a vehicle for bringing change to their respective continental union and the world.

The strategic objective to hold conferences that provide opportunities for community building, inspiration, training and celebration was achieved through the seven continental union assemblies. There were 3,426 women representing 117 countries that participated in these meetings. The Asian Baptist Women's Union was the fifth continental union to celebrate fifty years of ministry.

The Women's Department Executive Board worked hard on planning the 2010 Women's Leadership Conference. The theme was "In Step with the Spirit."

Social Ministry is an area of the Women's Department ministry designed to create awareness of, and also to meet, specific human needs. The following are achievements in this area.

During the past five years, seventeen projects have been undertaken in fifteen different countries. Some of the projects have benefited women and children socially and economically, and others have involved the training of women in practical ways and in theological education.

Corporate Identity is an area of priority related to making known the distinctive ministry of the Women's Department. The following are achievements in this area.

The BWA Women's Department website has been a creative and up to date way to tell the Women's Department story to young and old alike. It is also through the website that the e-newsletter, *Together for the Whole World,* is published. We have gone from publishing four editions in 2005 to publishing five editions in 2009.

Over a number of years, work has been done to prepare an updated history of the BWA Women's Department. In 2007, Esther Barnes was asked to write the Women's Department history. It was presented at the Baptist Women's Leadership Conference in Honolulu, Hawai`i.

At the 2008 BWA Women's Department Executive Board meeting, the organization's operational plan was reviewed and updated to reflect the work for 2008-2012. Joyce Wyatt was the Board's facilitator in the discussion and the updating.

The Women's Department world pendant trademark license was renewed. It continues to be a piece of jewelry that identifies Baptist women who pray for women around the world.

Development of Resources is an area of priority related to discovering, developing and sharing the various resources needed to achieve our mission. The following are achievements in this area.

The Day of Prayer offerings support the continental and worldwide ministries of the BWA Women's Department. The first part of the quinquennium showed a steady increase in the offerings, but towards the end there was a noticeable decline due to the world economic situation.

The funds from the Kindred Spirit appeal have helped in the printing of the Day of Prayer program, and aided other special projects such as leadership training in some of the continental unions and the publishing of two books. For the past two years, all funds have been designated for scholarships to the Women's Leadership Conference. Women responded enthusiastically, which helped to make it possible for the mission of the Women's Department to be achieved.

This report reflects the achievements in the four strategic areas of the Women's Department Operation Plan. There are still many more strategic objectives that need to be addressed. As we begin to be "In Step with the Spirit" may we stand together, grow in effectiveness, and impact our world for Christ.

Men in Ministry

At the BWA Centennial Congress, the BWA Men's Movement hosted a rally with more than 1,200 men participating. At this meeting, they installed new officers: Forestal Lawton as president, Harold Wolgast as secretary and Glenn Chelf as treasurer.

Each year during the 2005-2010 quinquennium, the men have conducted a Men's World Day of Prayer on the last Saturday in April. This has been a time for men around the world to gather and pray for their common concerns.

BWA men provided disaster relief training after Hurricane Katrina hit parts of the United States, especially the states of Louisiana and Mississippi in 2005, and after the January 12, 2010, earthquake in Haiti. They also undertook a renovation and construction project at Midwestern Seminary Chapel in Kansas City, Missouri, in the USA. They engaged in "discipleship making" and evangelism training meetings.

In 2006 and 2007, representatives of the BWA men attended the annual meeting of the Baptist Union of Great Britain in Swanwick, England, and of the Jamaica Baptist Union Brotherhood in 2008.

The men also participated in their regular March Executive meetings and the BWA Annual Gatherings. They looked forward to another men's rally that was held at the 2010 Congress in Hawai`i, when they installed new officers to continue to lead the work of the BWA Men's Department.

Evangelism and Education

During the quinquennium, the program of evangelism and education rotated around five major emphases.

Baptist Fund for World Evangelization and Discipleship (BFWED)

In fulfillment of its purpose to motivate BWA member bodies to carry out Christ's mandate of evangelism and discipleship, the Baptist Fund for World Evangelization and Discipleship (BFWED) provided twenty-one grants to member bodies in Bangladesh, Cambodia, Cameroon, Democratic Republic of Congo, India, Mozambique, Nepal, Papua New Guinea, Portugal, Sudan, the Caribbean, and Uganda.

Projects supported by BFWED include: grass roots evangelism efforts; church planting; translation and printing of study materials into native languages; leadership development and support; provision of Bibles; and Christian and theological education.

Baptist International Conference on Theological Education (BICTE VII)

BICTE serves as a forum for Baptist theologians around the world to engage in meaningful theological reflection as well as in worship and fellowship opportunities together. Following an established cycle, BICTE VII was held July 26-30, 2008, on the campus of the International Baptist Theological Seminary in Prague, the Czech Republic.

As a part of the preparations for the observance of the quadricentennial of the Baptist movement, BICTE VII gathered 121 participants from thirty-four countries to focus on the theme, "Probing the Theological Boundaries: The Baptist Story from Amsterdam to Tomorrow." *Perspectives in Religious Studies*, which is the journal of the National Association of Baptist Professors of Religion in the United States, published some of the BICTE VII papers in its summer 2009 issue.

The Emerging Leaders Network provides emerging Baptist leaders with a window to the Baptist movement worldwide and an opportunity for active involvement in the ministries of the BWA. During the quinquennium, 30 young Baptist leaders from 20 countries participated in ELN. At the group's initial sessions in Accra, Ghana, in 2007, these younger leaders made a four year commitment to participate in the ELN. At the end of the Ghana meetings, they issued a statement entitled, "Our vision for the BWA."

They convened again during the Annual Gatherings in Prague and Ede, attending and participating in Evangelism & Education Workgroup and Study & Research Commission sessions, as well as BWA worship services, committee meetings, forums and affinity groups, many serving as participant, presenter, or leader. The ELN were among the first to present a contribution to the BWA 400 Legacy Fund at the Annual Gathering in Ede, Netherlands.

Launched in Birmingham, England, on the occasion of the BWA Centennial Congress in July 2005, Christ the Living Water is a strategic plan designed to enlist and to equip local Baptists for evangelism and servant leadership. Since its inception, 19 Living Water events have taken place in the following countries: Australia, Bahamas, Bangladesh, Barbados, Brazil, the Czech Republic, Cuba, India, Kenya, Mozambique, Nepal, Nigeria, Panama, Russia, Serbia, Singapore, Sri Lanka, and Thailand.

In the years since the Birmingham launch, more than 4,600 registered delegates have participated in focused Bible study, evangelism and leadership training and prayer. Along with the thousands of worshippers attending the evening celebrations, participants in Living Water events have also reflected on the state of evangelistic endeavor in their own areas, re-committed their lives to the proclamation of the Good News of Christ Jesus, and have been encouraged to devise plans to pursue their evangelistic goals in order to meet the challenge to do evangelism in their local area.

The Baptist World Alliance has provided much needed theological literature to worthy and needy recipients – theological institutions, pastors and seminarians in the Global South through the Mini-Library Program. Each Mini-Library set contains an average of fourteen books determined to be essential in Christian theological education.

Since 2005, thirty-three sets of books have been shipped to Ghana, India, Kenya, Liberia, Mozambique, Myanmar, Nepal, the Philippines, South Africa, Zambia, and Zimbabwe.

Study and Research

Four major projects were undertaken during the quienquennium.

A new five-year cycle of theological conversations began in December 2006 between the Baptist World Alliance and the Pontifical Council for Promoting Christian Unity of the Roman Catholic Church. This series, with the theme, "The Word of God in the Life of the Church: Scripture, Tradition and Koinonia," concludes in December 2010.

As Baptists and Catholics face the challenges of today's world, they explore common ground in biblical teaching, apostolic faith and practical Christian living, as well as areas of division. Theological conversations are aiding mutual understanding, appreciation and Christian charity.

The Baptist and Catholic delegations have met at Beeson Divinity School, Birmingham, Alabama, USA (2006); Duke Divinity School, Durham, North Carolina, USA (2008), and Domus Internationalis Paulus VI, Rome, Italy (2007 and 2009).

To ensure gathering of information vital to the Baptist World Alliance, a document entitled, "Revised Procedures for Compiling Annual BWA Statistics", was produced and implemented in 2008. Statistics forms were made available by e-mail, postal service and on the BWA website in French, English, Portuguese and Spanish.

At the end of the quinquennium, the following statistics apply to the BWA:

- 219 member bodies in 120 countries
- 37,105,001 baptized members in 159,400 churches

Since the start of the quinquennium, BWA has grown by:

- 5 new member bodies
- 2,367,104 new baptized members
- 9,483 new churches

Baptist Identity

The Symposium on Baptist Identity held in Elstal, Germany, in March 2007, was attended by sixty-seven Baptist theologians, leaders and pastors from around the world.

The event focused on the autonomy of the local church as it relates to the wider community including associations, national conventions and unions, regional fellowships, and the BWA. The papers and declaration from the symposium have been published in German and are also available on the BWA website.

The aim of the Global Christian Forum is to promote dialogue, cooperation and common witness among all the main traditions in the Christian church worldwide. The BWA began its participation in the GCF Committee in 2006.

The GCF Committee held meetings in England, Finland, India, Kenya, and the Netherlands. Two hundred and forty-five delegates from seventy-two countries attended the Global Christian Forum event in Limuru, Kenya, November 6-9, 2007, under the theme, "Our Journey with Jesus Christ, the Reconciler." The papers from this forum were published in 2009 as *Revisioning Christian Unity: The Global Christian Forum* edited by Hubert van Beek. Information on the work of the Global Christian Forum is available at www.globalchristianforum.org.

Freedom and Justice

The Division on Freedom and Justice (F&J) was launched on September 1, 2008. Since then, F&J has worked to expand the BWA's impact in relation to religious freedom and other human rights issues. The first director of the Division on Freedom and Justice began serving in March 2010 and is helping galvanize our efforts before the world stage regarding human rights and justice issues among Baptists.

The BWA is a nongovernmental organization in consultative status with the United Nations Economic and Social Council and a member of the Conference of Non-Governmental Organizations in Consultative Relationship with the United Nations. Obtained in 1974, consultative status gives the BWA a higher level of access to all parts of the UN and the privilege of circulating its views to the General Assembly and the various commissions. Efforts have been made to better utilize our consultative status including BWA staff participation in meetings at the UN headquarters in New York City. A formal process for finding volunteers for the BWA's 22 United Nations seats worldwide was initiated and three such seats are currently filled.

For more than 20 years, the Baptist World Alliance has encouraged Baptist congregations around the world to observe Human Rights Day. The date coincides with the anniversary of the Universal Declaration of Human Rights that was adopted on December 10, 1948. In 2008 and 2009, supporting the ongoing tradition of BWA Human Rights Day, the new division posted worship resources on the BWA website and encouraged local churches to observe the day.

The F&J office has made significant progress in identifying potential partner organizations and individuals. Included in the list of potential partners are various Christian World Communions active in defense of religious liberty, as well as other international human rights organizations. Of particular interest are the opportunities presented through appropriate collaboration with the Office of International Religious Freedom of the United States Department of State and the United States Commission on International Religious Freedom.

The Denton and Janice Lotz Human Rights Award was presented during BWA Annual Gatherings from 2006-2009. The recipients were: Gustavo Parajon from Nicaragua, for his relief and development work; Joao and Nora Matwawana from Angola, for their role in reconciliation and peace efforts in Africa; Dennis Dilip Datta for his advocacy for Bangladesh independence, the restoration of democracy, and the establishment of religious freedom in his country; and Leena Lavanya from India, for her philanthropic work, human rights advocacy, and church planting endeavors.

The BWA General Council passed numerous freedom and justice-related resolutions during the quinquennium. Pertinent resolutions included statements on: violence against women and children, human rights abuses in Myanmar, the 200th anniversary of the passing of the Act to Abolish the Slave Trade in the British Colonies, Darfur, detention and due process, involuntary fingerprinting of Roma People in Italy, climate change, Zimbabwe, Baptist-Muslim relations, and religious freedom violations in Azerbaijan.

The BWA made several human rights visits during the past quinquennium, advocating for basic human rights for Baptists and other individuals throughout the world. In 2006 a human rights visit was made to Vietnam. The delegation, led by President David Coffey, sought to address human rights concerns, and in particular, religious freedom, in the Southeastern Asian country. The BWA president also appealed to Israeli and Palestinian leaders to give greater freedom to Christians during a visit in 2007. In January 2009, a European Baptist Federation/BWA delegation traveled to Azerbaijan. They met with a government committee on religion, members of the Baptist union, diplomatic representatives, and leaders of other religious groups to discuss human rights abuses and especially restrictions on religious liberty.

The BWA's Communications Division issues numerous releases on freedom and justice-related issues to inform Baptists of situations requiring prayer and action.

Relief and Development

From the Asian Tsunami (December 26, 2004) to the Haitian Earthquake (January 12, 2010)

Probably, BWAid has never had a year quite like 2005. The Asian tsunami, though dating back to December 26, 2004, manifested itself mostly in 2005. Major hurricanes, such as Katrina, caused loss of life and did untold damage in the Americas, as did the tragic earthquake in both Pakistan and Indian-controlled Kashmir. BWAid made grants amounting to $2,161,057.

2005 also saw the development of the BWAid Rescue24 teams.

Much of the focus in **2006** was around the Millennium Development Goals (MDGs), with each of the ninety-three BWAid projects focusing on the MDGs. Focusing on Hunger, BWAid worked with the Baptist Center for Ethics, in the production of a DVD, "Always...Therefore."

Although there were few major disasters during the year, it was recognized that any disaster is a major one to those caught up in it. BWAid grants totaled $1,870,922.

In **2007** there were no large "photogenic disasters." BWAid did, however, increase the training offered in Disaster Risk Management and Rapid Response (BWAid Rescue24).

In **2008** BWAid work was focused on Myanmar relief following Cyclone Nargis. The tragic restrictions imposed by the Burmese government in not allowing relief workers to enter the country meant that the people suffered even more. BWAid and other Baptist agencies worked together, supporting each other in their work and drawing together national and foreign leadership. $1,542,972 was awarded to various projects.

2009 appeared to be a year without major disasters. Unfortunately, it showed that our donors give more generously when there are larger and photogenic disasters. Much needed routine work and smaller development projects do not attract large donations, but BWAid gave $707,537 to a number of projects, while continuing to develop and promote the Millennium Development Goals. It is encouraging that many do give an annual donation for the relief of hunger.

So many disasters seem to happen at the beginning of the year, and so it came as no surprise that the tragic earthquake in Haiti happened on **January 12, 2010**. BWAid quickly started work and, within 24 hours, Rescue24 members were on their way from Hungary, joining other team members from North Carolina. The frustration of a 24 hour delay in getting to Port-au-Prince due to flight restrictions was soon overcome. Soon, contacts were made with the two BWA member bodies in Haiti, and North American relief groups have held roundtable conferences as longer term plans are being developed.

2010 has proven to be a hectic time as BWAid and other Baptist agencies have responded to the Haitian earthquake. BWAid has provided immediate relief funds, sent medical personnel and assisted with a shipment of medical supplies, assisted children with their feeding and education and given to help the needy.

In the four months from January 12 to May 19, BWAid received more than $1,177,000, spent $241,290, and made commitments of $430,000. A major project is now underway in one of the poorest areas of Port-au-Prince to provide an orphanage, school, cafeteria, and community facilities. BWAid recognizes that Haiti will most likely demand the majority of our time for the rest of the year.

BWAid seeks to use the funds received as prudently and expeditiously as possible. Tsunami funds were still being dispersed in 2009, and Haiti earthquake funds will be used in the years ahead as we try to ensure that care is provided for the Haitians in the years ahead. Grants awarded by BWAid totaled $1,406,799 in 2010.

Promotion and Development

At the start of the 2005-2010 quinquennium, the BWA had just come out of a downturn in the world's economic markets and had completed its largest fundraising effort to date, purchasing a new physical facility, with $1.5 million dollars from three individuals whose gifts were supplemented by another $300,000 from member bodies and individual supporters. In contrast, a 20 percent budget reduction for the BWA in 2004 had led to a serious re-thinking of the ways in which individuals and institutions are encouraged to relate to the BWA, and to the development of strategic new ways of encouraging financial support for the BWA.

Promotion and Development (P&D) is charged with the responsibility of finding additional and stabilizing support sources for the BWA at a time when the organization is implementing new approaches to ministry that emerged from the report of the Twenty-First Century Committee. During this quinquennium, P&D passed through a three-year period in which a director of Advancement provided oversight and leadership for both P&D and Communications.

During the quinquennium, marked by years of change and challenge, P&D has sought to respond with imagination, flexibility, and immediacy to the developing resource needs of the organization. Work has been done diligently and purposefully under the leadership of the general secretary to gain and retain loyal support and to secure meaningful avenues through which BWA supporters may more easily express partnership and oneness with the organization.

Arising from consultation with the P&D Committee, 10 key strategies were employed during this quinquennium:

- Developing strong branding of BWA as a Baptist network with use of logos
- Using fewer but more effective appeals
- Engaging younger Baptists in BWA life
- Instituting a coordinated planned giving program

- Offering online giving opportunity
- Positioning BWA as the Baptist leader on Freedom and Justice
- Increasing use of new technologies (web, emails, blogs, etc.)
- Using communications vehicles for appeals (magazine, newsletter, etc.)
- Providing a new brochure – a "view book" with coordinating DVD
- Coordinating communication with fund raising strategies

The following are 25 key accomplishments during this quinquennium:

- Received service mark status for "Your network to the world!" logo (registration approved 2009) for use on all materials as part of our branding effort
- Consolidated and targeted appeals (from 11 to 6 key annual appeals)
- Generated interest in the BWA from more than 1,400 young Baptists (starting with Texas Baptists but expanding internationally) who signed our petition for Freedom and Justice, the majority of whom continue to receive updates on our work
- Created a long-awaited multi-tiered Planned Giving program with brochures, a website and weekly e-newsletters on topics of interest to donors who may consider end-of-life gifts and other major provisions for the BWA
- Gained approval to solicit an annual offering from Baptist churches
- Instituted online giving on our website
- Furnished a BWA video studio for distributing messages and videos via the web and DVDs
- Produced an introductory DVD for churches and organizations on the incoming general secretary
- Produced a new general brochure and a 7.5-minute DVD outlining the general mission of the BWA emphasizing our ministries in the five clusters of commitment
- Encouraged church support by instituting:
  - a twice-yearly Pastors Coffee for Washington Metro area pastors
  - Wednesday Prayer emails to encourage congregations to pray with us for Baptists around the world
  - new pathways for churches and pastors to relate to us with a World Impact Pastors blog, and

- offers of mission opportunities in North America and elsewhere
- Contributed to a re-purposed BWA newsletter from Communications creating a cooperative vehicle for promotion of the Baptist World Alliance
- Assisted in securing a $1,000,000-plus gift over five years for Living Water, an evangelism initiative
- Grew the Global Impact Church initiative to include Global Partners and Participating Churches as donor recognition programs, expanding from a charter group of 124 Global Impact Churches in 2004 to a total of more than 700 donor churches of all types supporting our mission
- Helped raise $5,646,350.49 in church donations for the Baptist World Alliance overall from 2004-2009
- Raised $125,000 for a special award fund for Freedom and Justice recognition
- Organized and directed a five-week, twenty-one-city tour of North America for the new general secretary to introduce himself to USA Baptist groups and leaders
- Re-envisioned the BWA Ambassadors program and enlisted 150+ Ambassadors by 2009 to help promote the BWA among churches and individuals
- Launched the Emerita/Emeritus Club to retain support and input from former BWA executives
- Launched the 400 Legacy Fund as a reserve fund to secure the stability of programs and initiatives of the BWA during difficult economic times
- Invited all Baptists to participate in global Baptist work by giving a 400 Thank Offering recognizing 400 years of Baptist heritage which received to date $27,815.53 in direct gifts to the 400 Legacy Fund (this initiative continues through 2015)
- Instituted the 400 Legacy Society as a recognition for those donating to the 400 Legacy Fund or in end-of-life gifts for the future ministries of the BWA
- Created new large display banners, brochures, presentations, etc., to present the BWA image and message visually
- Provided a strong BWA presence at two dozen or more member body meetings to show support and fellowship

- Continued to secure strong support from churches and individuals during the worst economic downturn in 40 years
- Received excellent collaboration from Communications and other ministries of the BWA to achieve these accomplishments

Certainly, more challenges lie ahead and we will continue to implement programs to reach supporters of a new generation. These are the Baptists of the 21st century and many wish to relate to us in new, perhaps non-institutional, ways. At the same time, we embrace the previous generations who have provided the means for the BWA's ministries to expand to this point. The BWA recognizes the need for both the wisdom of the previous century as well as that of future Baptists in order to garner the financial partnerships that will see this movement evolve to the next level of fellowship in its second century of service. We anticipate the sacrifices that our member organizations and churches will make for the work ahead.

The economic recovery that we hope for may be slow in coming, but the BWA enjoys the loyalty and commitment of Baptist churches and member bodies that will support the worldwide Baptist family even in times of struggle. In 2009, we still gained support from one additional seminary and 12 churches gave to the BWA for the first time. Sixty individuals also made first time donations to the BWA.

We have a growing number of BWA Ambassadors encouraging individuals and churches who see their ministries and each other as part of this global fellowship, and we have the past officers of the BWA and its member organizations loyally demonstrating their continued commitment to the body as Emeriti. We have the promise of a gracious God to provide all we need to accomplish God's will for us.

It has been a quinquennium with challenges and miracles, and we look with confidence to the next five years as we collaborate with each ministry to serve the Baptists of the world. We will continue to see God's guidance and to urge Baptists to joyfully affirm our oneness and enthusiastically share in the privilege of participating in God's mission.

Communications

Over the quinquennium, there has been an increase in the utilization of new media and communications technology in the execution of the functions of the communications portfolio.

The **website** has been through two new designs to enhance function and appearance and to meet the growing needs of the organization, such as the ability to accept donations online. The newsletter, now known as *BWA Connect*, is primarily produced in electronic format since April 2007. The magazine, *Baptist World*, saw an increase in the number of pages from twenty-four to thirty-two and became an ezine as of October 2008. As a consequence, the numbers of the printed copies of both the newsletter and the magazine have been drastically reduced.

The BWA has run several blogs, and established Twitter and Facebook accounts.

In addition to the newsletter and magazine, the division produced or helped to organize the production of five issues of a congress newspaper in Birmingham, and two newsletters at the Baptist Youth World Conference in Leipzig. Beginning in 2007, the division has been responsible for the production of the BWA calendar.

Training seminars have been held at every Annual Gathering over the past five years with focus on electronic media, broadcast media, print media, crisis management, and preparing press releases, among other subjects.

In addition, training sessions were conducted in Trinidad in July 2006 at the Caribbean Baptist Fellowship Assembly; at the Jamaica Baptist Union Assembly in Jamaica in February 2007; and in Chiang Mai, Thailand, at the Asia Baptist Congress in May 2007. These sessions were in response to requests made to the office.

Great emphasis is placed on reporting on, and reporting to, the Baptist constituency around the world. As such, a great deal of information is gathered, much of it from primary sources around the world, that is shared through press releases. Three hundred and forty-two press releases were issued - 40 in 2005; 52 in 2006; 84 in 2007; 80 in 2008; and 86 in 2009.

The division organized and hosted press conferences at the Centenary Congress in Birmingham, England, in 2005; the Annual Gathering in Prague, Czech Republic, in 2008; the Baptist Youth World Conference in Leipzig, Germany, in 2008; and on the occasion of the dedication of the Baptism Center in Amman, Jordan, in March 2009.

The division ran press rooms at the Centenary Congress in Birmingham in 2005 and at the Baptist Youth World Conference in Leipzig, Germany, 2008. There were 112 accredited media persons from 20 countries at the Centenary Congress, including fifteen official BWA reporters.

A digital photo library has been established. Collating and cataloguing files is an ongoing process with many thousands of photos already processed.

A video recording studio is in the process of being established and has been used in the production of several videos, including messages by the general secretary.

Personnel Changes

At the end of the last quinquennium in 2005, we lost two long-serving members of the BWA Executive staff, Tony Cupit, E&E, S&R Director, and Wendy Ryan, Communications Director.

Since the start of the quinquennium, several changes took place in the BWA Executive staff.

The following Executive staff members retired from the BWA:

- Denton Lotz, BWA General Secretary, August 2007
- Ellen Teague, Finance and Administration Director, December 2009

The following Executive staff members resigned from the BWA:

- Elizabeth Wright, Associate Director for Promotion and Development, June 2006
- Ron Harris, Mission Advancement Director, July 2006
- Ian Chapman, Special Assistant to the General Secretary, July 2007
- Alan Stanford, Mission Advancement Director, August 2008

Executive staff replacements were provided as follows:

- Eron Henry, Associate Director for Communications, January 2006
- Fausto Vasconcelos, Evangelism & Education, Study & Research Director, June 2006
- Katherine Traynham, Associate Director for Promotion & Development, January 2007
- Nina Neubauer, Executive Assistant to General Secretary, January 2007
- Neville Callam, General Secretary, September 2007
- Margaret Pearson, Comptroller, January 2010
- Raimundo Barreto, Freedom and Justice Director, March 2010
- Don Sewell completed a one-year contract as BWA Fundraiser, September 2009

Of course, Emmett Dunn, Patsy Davis and Paul Montacute continue to serve as BWA directors for the Youth and Women's Departments, and BWAid, respectively.

The quinquennium is memorable as a time marked by many administrative changes and adjustments arising out of the work of the Twenty-First Century Committee and the Implementation Task Force. Several changes were made to the BWA Bylaws. Several other administrative changes were introduced. With their velocity and timing, these changes posed severe challenges especially for BWA Executive staff members assuming new responsibilities.

Publications

During the quinquennium, several publications were undertaken by BWA staff.

Baptist World was issued quarterly.

BWA Connect has been issued monthly since November 2008, as successor to BWA News

Together for the Whole World, a newsletter of the BWA Women's Department, published quarterly in electronic form

Tony Cupit's *Living Water Bible Study Book* and *Biblical Models for Evangelism* appeared in English, Bengali, French, Nepalese, New Guinea Pidgin, Portuguese, Serbian, Sinhalese, Spanish, and Tamil

Telling the Story, edited by Tony Cupit, which resulted from the workshops at the Living Water Conference in Birmingham, England, July 2005, offers specific approaches to sharing the Good News of God's love in Jesus Christ with specific groups of people

Baptist Faith & Witness Book 3, edited by Tony Cupit, with papers presented at S&R Commission meetings during the last quinquennium

Perspectives in Religious Studies, Vol. 36, No. 2, Summer 2009, contained some of the BICTE VII papers. *Perspectives in Religious Studies* is the journal of the National Association of Baptist Professors of Religion in the United States

Joyce Cope Wyatt, *I am a woman...Created in the Image of God* (English Title) *Soy Mujer! Soy Especial!* (Spanish original)

Esther Barnes, *Coming Together: A History of the Women's Department*

Neville Callam, *Pursuing Unity and Defending Rights in the Baptist World Alliance*

A Celebration of Christian Service: Reflections from BWA Staff, edited by Eron Henry, contains reflections on aspects of the ministry of the BWA

Baptists against Racism: Reflections at the End of a Decade, edited by Neville Callam & Julie Justus – a compendium of statements against racism issued by the BWA over the years, being published to mark the end of the Decade against Racism and Ethnic Conflict

Reporting the Baptist News: Selected Articles from Baptist World Magazine, edited by Eron Henry, essential stories and reflections published in Baptist World during the current quinquennium

Acknowledgement

We owe grateful thanks to God for the opportunity to share in the work of the BWA, for the partnership and collaboration that make this work possible, and for the enabling that the Holy Spirit ceaselessly supplies.

20. In Memoriam, 2005-2010

2005

Name	Country
Roy Honeycutt	USA (died in 2004, not previously listed)
Akiko Matsumura	Japan
Kerstin Ruden	Sweden
Arthur Walker	USA

2006

Name	Country
Piero Bensi	Italy
Rode Dubelzars	USA
Wes Forsline	USA
Rodney Gordon	Belize
Wenzao Han	China
William A. Jones	USA
Franjo Klem	Former Yugoslavia
Policarpo Peréz Leyva	Cuba
Phil Strickland	USA
Foy Valentine	USA
Grace Widjaja	Indonesia

2007

Name	Country
Frank Adams	Ghana
William Cumbie	USA
Wayne Dehoney	USA
Darci Dusilek	Brazil
Sam Fadeji	Nigeria
Ruth Graham	USA
William J. Harvey, III	USA
Gennadi Konstantinovich Krychkov	Russia
Hans-Harald Mallau	Germany
Azariah McKenzie	Jamaica
John Merritt	USA
Wiard Popkes	Germany
J. Ralph McIntyre	USA
Jose Missena	Paraguay
Herb Reynolds	USA
Sailendra Kumar Sen	India
Jack Snell	USA
Waldemiro Tymchak	Brazil
Norman Adrian Wiggins	USA

2008

Name	Country
Daniel T.K. Baroi	Bangladesh
C. Howard Bentall	Canada
C.W. Brister	USA
Bernadette Cakpo	Benin
O. Judith Chambers	Canada

David Charley	United Kingdom
Edna Lee de Gutiérrez	Mexico
Alma Hunt	USA
Vicky O'Boyle	USA
Dellanna O'Brien	USA
Walter Pulliam	USA
David T. Shannon	USA
W.G. Wickremasinghe	Sri Lanka
David Wong	Hong Kong

2009

Name	Country
Yenny Abril	Ecuador
Jan Bowman	New Zealand
Robert Campbell	USA
Winston Clemetson	Jamaica
Thomas Corts	USA
Stewart Cleveland Cureton	USA
Nilson do Amaral Fanini	Brazil
John H. Foster	USA
Lilian Lim Hui Kiau	Singapore
Vasili Logvinenko	Russia
Ondina Maristany	Cuba
Roger Martin	United Kingdom
Alfred Peck	United Kingdom
Simon H. Sircar	Bangladesh
Peter Tongeman	United Kingdom
Philip Wise	USA

2010

Name	Country
C. Bill Hogue	USA
Sydney Hudson-Reed	South Africa
Davorin Peterlin	Croatia
Klaus Pritzkuleit	Germany
Cecil Sherman	USA
John Smith	New Zealand
Edwin Tuller	USA

21. CONSTITUTION OF THE BAPTIST WORLD ALLIANCE

AS AMENDED BY THE GENERAL COUNCIL

EDE, NETHERLANDS

JULY 2009

PREAMBLE

The Baptist World Alliance, extending over every part of the world, exists as an expression of the essential oneness of Baptist people in the Lord Jesus Christ, to impart inspiration to the fellowship, and to provide channels for sharing concerns and skills in witness and ministry. This Alliance recognizes the traditional autonomy and interdependence of Baptist churches and member bodies.

I. NAME

This organization shall be known as the Baptist World Alliance, hereinafter referred to as "the Alliance."

II. OBJECTIVES

Under the guidance of the Holy Spirit, the objectives of the Alliance shall be:

1. To promote Christian fellowship and cooperation among Baptists throughout the world.
2. To bear witness to the gospel of Jesus Christ and assist member bodies in their divine task of bringing all people to God through Jesus Christ as Savior and Lord.
3. To promote understanding and cooperation among Baptist bodies and with other Christian groups, in keeping with our unity in Christ.
4. To act as an agency for the expression of Biblical faith and historically distinctive Baptist principles and practices.
5. To act as an agency of reconciliation seeking peace for all persons, and uphold the claims of fundamental human rights, including full religious liberty.
6. To serve as a channel for expressing Christian social concern and alleviating human need.
7. To serve in cooperation with member bodies as a resource for the development of plans for evangelism, education, church growth, and other forms of mission.
8. To provide channels of communication dealing with work related to these objectives through all possible media.

III. METHOD OF OPERATIONS

The Alliance shall operate throughout the world through:

1. The Baptist World Congress
2. The General Council
3. The Executive Committee
4. Its Officers
5. Such committees and organizational structures as are provided for in the Bylaws or as authorized by the General Council.
6. Regional Fellowships or Federations

IV. MEMBERSHIP

1. An organized Baptist body such as a union or convention which desires to cooperate in the work of the Alliance shall be eligible for membership, subject to the approval of the General Council. In accepting membership in the Alliance the member body thereby assumes responsibility for assisting in the support and furtherance of the purposes and work of the Alliance.

2. ASSOCIATE MEMBERSHIP: The intention of Associate Membership is to involve Baptist churches and organized Baptist groups in the global ministry of the Baptist World Alliance through prayer, the sharing of resources and participation in the meetings, congresses and conferences of the Baptist World Alliance. The ministry of churches, organized Baptist bodies and the Alliance are all strengthened through this intentional partnership.

3. PERSONAL MEMBERSHIP: The intention of Personal Membership is to involve Baptists in the global ministry of the Baptist World Alliance through prayer, the sharing of resources and participation in the meetings, congresses and conferences of the Baptist World Alliance. The ministry of individuals and the Alliance are both strengthened through this intentional partnership

V. BAPTIST WORLD CONGRESS

1. The Alliance shall normally assemble in a Baptist World Congress once in five years for the purpose of fellowship, inspiration, information, enrichment, encouragement, and required business.

2. The Congress shall be comprised of members of churches which belong to a member body of the Alliance.

VI. GENERAL COUNCIL

The General Council shall comprise:
1. (a) The President, the Vice-Presidents, the General Secretary and the Treasurer;

(b) Members nominated by member bodies and seated by the General Council, vacancies to be
filled by the General Council on nomination of the member body concerned. The number of places to be allocated to each member body shall be determined in accordance with the Bylaws: provided that each member body shall be entitled to at least one place, and no member body shall have more than ten percent of the total membership of the Council.

(c)   The presiding officer and one additional representative of each Auxiliary and the Youth
Department and six ex-officio members representing the Auxiliaries and the Youth Department or equivalent entity in the regions nominated by the governing body of each Auxiliary and the Youth Department, and seated by the General Council. Vacancies are to be filled by the General Council on nomination of the Auxiliary concerned and the Youth Department.

(d) The chair of the following program divisions: Communication, Baptist World Aid, Evangelism and
Education, Study and Research, and Promotion and Development

(e)   The chair of standing committees

(f)   The presiding officer of each Regional Fellowship

2. Not more than twelve additional members, any of whom may be co-opted by the General Council at any time, to serve until the conclusion of the next Baptist World Congress. In making such co-options, the General Council shall give consideration to, but not be limited to, representation of the committees and organizational structures which assist the Alliance in the work.

3. Past Presidents and Past General Secretaries, who shall be life members.

VII. FUNCTIONS OF THE GENERAL COUNCIL

The General Council is served by the General Secretary as Chief Executive Officer. The Council expresses representative responsibility, conducts Alliance business, acts as a general forum, and undertakes such activities as those pertaining to the Constitution, Bylaws, Elections, Executive Staff, Policy, Program, Finance, Resolutions, Relationships, Research and History.

The General Council shall:

1. Transact the business of the Alliance between Baptist World Congresses and supervise the administration of any undertaking of the Alliance.
2. Appoint an Executive Committee as indicated in Article VIII below, and authorize such organizational structures and committees as it may deem necessary and determine their duties.
3. Arrange local, regional, continental, or other conferences as may be considered desirable.
4. Fill vacancies as provided in Article X of the Constitution.
5. Determine the time and place of the Baptist World Congress, and be responsible for all necessary arrangements, including the preparation of the program.
6. Serve as a Nominating Committee in respect to the election of the President, the Vice-Presidents and the Treasurer.
7. Elect the General Secretary and such other executive staff as the General Council may deem desirable. Executive staff members are elected with anticipation of service until the conclusion of the ensuing Baptist World Congress and may be re-elected.

VIII. EXECUTIVE COMMITTEE

There shall be an Executive Committee comprised of no more than twenty five persons appointed by the General Council from its membership. The Executive committee shall be comprised as follows: the President, the First Vice-President, the General Secretary, the Treasurer, the Immediate Past President, the President of the BWA Women's Auxiliary, the President of the BWA Youth Department, a representative of each BWA region appointed by that region and 12 at large representatives elected by the General Council from names submitted through the Nominations Committee with a desire to ensure an Executive Committee gifted in membership, global in representation and holistic in terms of female and male, young and old. The General Council at large representatives will be elected four each year for three year terms which are renewable. The Executive Committee will elect a Chairperson from its number to chair the meetings. The General Secretary reports to the Executive Committee. No member of the BWA staff may serve as a voting member of the Executive Committee except the General Secretary.

IX. FUNCTIONS OF THE EXECUTIVE COMMITTEE

Subject to the authority reserved to the General Council in accordance with Article VII of this Constitution and applicable laws, the business, property, affairs and funds of the Alliance shall be managed, supervised and controlled by the Executive Committee. The Executive Committee shall fulfil its oversight responsibilities in furtherance of the purposes and objectives of the Alliance and shall provide regular reports to the General Council regarding its deliberations and actions.

X. OFFICERS

The Officers of the Alliance shall be the President, the First Vice-President, up to eleven Vice-Presidents, the General Secretary and the Treasurer. The Baptist World Congress, upon nomination by the General Council, shall elect the President, the First Vice President, the Vice-Presidents, and the Treasurer whose terms of office shall be from the conclusion of one Baptist World Congress until the conclusion of the next.

The General Council shall elect the General Secretary.

If an officer should die, resign, or become incapable of acting, the General Council shall fill the vacancy and that officer shall serve until the conclusion of the next Baptist World Congress.

XI. REGIONAL FELLOWSHIPS or FEDERATIONS

1. A Regional Fellowship or Federation recognized by the Alliance shall be an association of organized autonomous Baptist bodies such as unions and conventions within a defined geographical area.

XII. AMENDMENTS

1. Amendments to the Constitution may be made by the General Council.

2. No change shall be made in this Constitution except by a two-thirds majority of General Council members present and voting, and shall require a year's Notice of Motion.

BYLAWS OF THE BAPTIST WORLD ALLIANCE
AS AMENDED BY THE GENERAL COUNCIL, EDE, NETHERLANDS, JULY 2009

ARTICLE I
MEMBERSHIP

1.   FULL MEMBERSHIP

a) A Baptist body applying for membership in the Baptist World Alliance (hereinafter the "BWA") shall authorize its applications for membership through its own due process and shall, either directly or through its officers or duly empowered committee, subscribe to the objectives and financial support of the BWA as set forth in the Constitution and Bylaws of the BWA.

b)   Each Baptist body which is accorded full membership (hereafter "Member Body") shall have an identity of its own and shall not exist as an integral part of some other union or convention.

c) The BWA Executive Committee shall, from time to time, determine the criteria and/or guidelines for membership, which the Membership Committee shall use to evaluate an application for membership submitted by a Member Body. Applications which are determined to meet membership requirements will be recommended by the Membership Committee to the Executive Committee for its action and recommendation to the General Council for approval.

d) Every Member Body shall assume responsibility, in its own sphere of influence, for the promotion of the BWA programs consistent with its own work.

e) Every Member Body shall assume a fair and reasonable share of financial support for the general work and programs of the BWA. In currency controlled countries, money spent in behalf of the BWA programs within the currency controlled area may be regarded as a contribution towards the Member Body's financial responsibilities to the BWA.

f) In order that the BWA may share information, each Member Body shall report to the BWA annual statistics on the number of churches and persons in its membership, based on careful reports or surveys of that membership. Further, the Member Body should report regularly to its constituency through its own publications and annual meetings on the ministry of the BWA.

2. ASSOCIATE MEMBERSHIP

a) Baptist churches may be admitted as an Associate Member of the Baptist World Alliance

b) Organized Baptist groups (e.g. colleges, universities, seminaries, mission organizations, state, regional or associational divisions of member or non-member Baptist bodies, historical societies, etc.) may be admitted as an Associate Member of the BWA.

c) Associate Members of the BWA will demonstrate their support by paying an appropriate annual membership fee as determined by the Executive Committee upon recommendation by the Budget and Finance Committee.

d) All Associate Membership applications will be reviewed by the Membership Committee and reported to the Executive Committee and the General Council.

3.   PERSONAL MEMBERSHIP

a)   Individual Baptists may become personal members of the BWA by paying an appropriate annual membership fee determined by the Executive Committee upon recommendation by the Budget and Finance Committee.

b) All Personal Membership applications will be reviewed by the Membership Committee and reported to the Executive Committee and to the General Council.

ARTICLE II
GENERAL COUNCIL

1.   MEMBERSHIP

a) Each Member Body shall be entitled to representation on the General Council under clause (1) (b) of Article VI of the Constitution as follows: One representative for each Member Body of up to 40,000 church members; two (2) for each Member Body with 40,000 or more church members, up to 200,000; three (3) for each Member Body with 200,000 or more church members, up to 1,000,000; and four (4) for Member Bodies with over 1,000,000 church members.

b) Member Bodies of 5,000,000 and more members may appoint one (1) additional member for each full million above that number.

c) Member Bodies are encouraged to include laypersons, women, men, and youth, in the appointments listed above.

d) Additionally, Member Bodies appointing two (2) members of Council may appoint a third, provided that the third person is a female, a layperson, or a youth (under 35 years of age at the time of the appointment).

e) Member Bodies appointing three (3) members to the Council may appoint two additional members, provided they represent two of the three groups mentioned.

f) Member Bodies appointing four (4) or more members to the Council may appoint three more, provided they represent each of the three groups mentioned.

g) An additional ten (10) places in total shall be allocated among Member Bodies of fewer than five million members, taking into account their interest in and support of the BWA. Such allocations shall be made by the Executive Committee and approved by the General Council in sufficient time to permit the Member Bodies to nominate their representatives prior to the beginning of the term of office.

h) Three (3) at-large members shall be co-opted to serve on the General Council to represent all churches, institutions and individuals that have been accepted as Associate and Personal members.   These at-large members shall be nominated by the Nominations Committee and elected by the General Council.

i) The General Secretary shall serve as an ex-officio voting member of the   General Council and all Committees of the General Council. No other member of the BWA staff, whether based in the BWA offices or in the regions, may serve as a member of the General Council or its Committees

2. MEETINGS

Normally the General Council meets once a year upon the call of the General Secretary. A meeting may also be called upon the written request of fifteen of its members delivered to the President and /or the General Secretary. Written notice of any meeting shall be communicated to every member of the General Council at least three months before the proposed meeting date.

3. QUORUM

Fifty (50) members shall constitute a quorum for the transaction of business provided that at least fifteen (15) Member Bodies are represented.

4. MANNER OF ACTING

Unless otherwise provided by the Articles of Incorporation or these Bylaws, if a quorum is present at a meeting of the Council, the affirmative vote of a majority of the Council shall be the act of the Council.

5. PROXIES

A Member Body, a Regional Fellowship or Federation, or an Auxiliary of the BWA may appoint a proxy for a General Council member who is unable to represent it at a meeting of the Council. Notice of an appointment of proxy shall be delivered to the General Secretary in writing at least one month prior to the General Council meeting. Such proxies have the right to vote. Members of the General Council may not serve as proxies.

6. PROCEEDINGS

a) Persons who are not members of the General Council may generally attend open meetings of the General Council, provided that only members of the General Council may participate in discussion, unless a non-member is requested by the President to participate in the meeting. The President may designate certain meetings "closed" to non-Council members.

b) General Council debate on resolutions coming from the Resolutions Committee shall follow guidelines developed by the Resolutions Committee and approved by the General Council. All such resolutions shall require the affirmative vote of a ¾ majority of Council members present and voting for adoption.

ARTICLE III
COMMITTEES OF THE GENERAL COUNCIL

1. COMMITTEES GENERALLY

The General Council will determine the authority and responsibility of each Committee of the General Council as set forth in a Committee Charter developed by the Executive Committee and approved by the General Council.

2. NOMINATIONS COMMITTEE

a) The Nominations Committee will assist the General Council and the Executive Committee by generating, receiving, reviewing and recommending names of persons eligible and willing to serve as officers, Executive Committee members and core members of Commissions as referenced in Article VII of these Bylaws. Nominations of appropriate persons to serve on these bodies will be subject to appointment by the General Council or Executive Committee in accordance with these Bylaws, Committee Charters and any other guidelines developed by the Executive Committee. Persons appointed will generally serve for a Quinquennium.

b) A key purpose of the Nominations Committee will be to ensure that the global reality of the BWA is represented on its Executive Committee and Commissions, and that the search for suitable qualified candidates will be as wide and as comprehensive as possible.

c) The membership of the Nominations Committee shall include: the President and the General Secretary, both of whom shall serve as ex officio voting members, three (3) members appointed by the General Council for the Quinquennium, and two (2) members nominated by the regional Council or any executive committee from each region. These persons shall not be members of the BWA staff.

d) The Committee shall appoint a chair from among its members. It meets upon the call of the General Secretary.

3. RESOLUTIONS COMMITTEE

a) The Resolutions Committee will assist the General Council by bringing resolutions to the General Council for consideration. The Committee shall be appointed by the General Council from recommendations submitted by the Nominations Committee. The Committee shall have not less than six and not more than twelve members.

b) All resolutions which BWA members wish to be considered by the General Council must be proposed to the Resolutions Committee.

ARTICLE IV
EXECUTIVE COMMITTEE

1. GENERAL POWERS

a) Subject to the authority reserved to the General Council in accordance with Article VII of the Constitution, and consistent with the functions of the Executive Committee set forth in Article IX of the Constitution, and applicable laws, the business, property, affairs and funds of the BWA shall be managed, supervised and controlled by the Executive Committee. The Executive Committee shall fulfill its oversight responsibilities in furtherance of the purposes and objectives of the BWA and shall function as the board of directors under applicable law. To fulfill the Executive Committee's oversight responsibilities, the Executive Committee shall initiate and establish organizational policies governing the operation and management of the BWA, and may appoint one or more committees as set forth in Article V of these Bylaws to assist it in carrying out its governance role.

b) In furtherance of its general oversight role, the Executive Committee shall be responsible for:
(i) overseeing the development and implementation of the overall program of the BWA based on the Clusters of Commitment adopted by the General Council and having regard for the overall direction of the General Council
(ii) receiving and reviewing reports, proposals and recommendations from the General Secretary on the activities and affairs of the BWA and taking action as appropriate;
(iii) generally overseeing the financial affairs of the BWA including: securing adequate funds to support the work of the BWA, approval of the annual budget and any subsequent revisions, ensuring financial

reporting that meets applicable regulatory requirements, and annually approving the selection of an external auditor;

(iv) receiving and reviewing reports and recommendations from Committees of the Executive Committee; and

(v) receiving and responding to initiatives and proposals from the auxiliaries.

2. COMPOSITION, APPOINTMENT AND TERMS

a) The composition of the Executive Committee and provisions regarding appointment and terms of Executive Committee members are set forth in Article VIII of the Constitution. The Executive Committee shall be appointed at the beginning of the Quinquennium. Members serve for the Quinquennium with the exception of those members appointed directly by the General Council who shall be appointed in groups of four for staggered 3 year terms, which terms are renewable. The Committee shall appoint a chair from among its members, who will normally be the President.

b) Vacancies created during the Quinquennium will be filled at the next General Council meeting.

c) The General Secretary shall serve as an ex-officio voting member of the Executive Committee and all Committees of the Executive Committee, and shall be the only staff member to serve in such capacity, whether based in the BWA offices or in the regions.

3. MEETINGS

a) The Executive Committee will meet at least two times annually. Regular Meetings of the Executive Committee shall be held at such time and at such location as determined by the Executive Committee. Special meetings of the Executive Committee may be called by the President or the General Secretary and shall be held at such time and at such location as determined by the President and General Secretary.

b) The members of the Executive Committee may participate in any meeting of the Executive Committee by means of conference telephone or similar communications equipment, provided all persons participating in the meeting can hear and speak to each other. Participation of an Executive Committee member by means of conference telephone or similar communications equipment shall constitute presence of the member in person at the meeting.

c) Written Notice of any Regular meeting shall be communicated to every member of the Executive Committee at least three months before the date of the proposed meeting. Written notice of any Special meeting shall be communicated to every member of the Executive Committee at least five (5) business days before the date of the proposed meeting.

4. ACTION WITHOUT A MEETING

Any action to be taken at a meeting of the Executive Committee may be taken without a meeting if a consent, in writing, setting forth the action so taken shall be signed by all of the Executive Committee members. Such consent shall have the same effect as a unanimous vote. A sign written consent may be accomplished by one or more electronic transmissions.

5. QUORUM

A majority of the Executive Committee shall constitute a quorum for the transaction of business at any meeting of the Executive Committee.

6. MANNER OF ACTING

Unless otherwise required by law, by the Articles of Incorporation, or by these Bylaws, if a quorum is present at a meeting of the Executive Committee, the affirmative vote of a majority of the Executive Committee present at the meeting shall be the act of the Executive Committee. No Executive Committee member shall act by proxy on any matter.

7. PROCEEDINGS

a) Persons who are not members of the Executive Committee may generally attend open meetings of the Executive Committee, provided that only members of the Executive Committee may participate in discussion, unless the Committee Chair requests that a non-member participate in the meeting for a specific purpose. Members of the BWA staff may attend at the specific request of the General Secretary.

b) The Committee Chair shall have the authority to designate certain meetings of the Executive

Committee "closed" to non-committee members upon the request of the President, the General Secretary or four members of the Executive Committee. The Executive Committee will authorize the General Secretary to make statements to the public on the proceedings of a closed session.

8. REPORTS TO THE GENERAL COUNCIL

The Executive Committee shall provide regular reports to the General Council regarding its deliberations and actions, and on other matters as may be requested by the General Council from time to time.

ARTICLE V
COMMITTEES OF THE EXECUTIVE COMMITTEE

1. COMMITTEES GENERALLY

a) The Executive Committee may establish one or more committees as needed or required to 2assist the Executive Committee in providing governance oversight of the activities and affairs of the BWA. The initial standing committees shall include, but not be limited to: Budget and Finance, Audit, Human Resources, Membership, Baptist World Congress and Baptist World Aid.

b) Each committee shall consist of at least two (2) members of the Executive Committee and an Executive Committee member will chair each committee. Committees may include persons other than members of the Executive Committee based on specific skills or expertise helpful to the committee in fulfilling its responsibilities. Committee members will be appointed by the Executive Committee taking into consideration any recommendations from the Nominations Committee.

c) The Executive Committee will determine the authority and responsibility of each committee as set forth in a Committee Charter developed and approved by the Executive Committee. The Charter will also identify committee size, composition based on identified skills and experience, and frequency of meetings. Minutes of all committee meetings shall be recorded and copies of such minutes shall be provided to the Executive Committee. In addition, each committee shall present a report covering its deliberations and actions to the Executive Committee at each of its meetings. Each committee will also make recommendations to the Executive Committee on matters requiring Executive Committee approval.

2. LIMITATIONS

No committee appointed by the Executive Committee shall be granted the authority of the Executive Committee to:

a) Amend, alter, or repeal the BWA Constitution or Bylaws;

b) Elect, appoint, or remove any member of any committee or officer of the BWA.

c) Amend the Articles of Incorporation, restate the Articles of Incorporation, adopt a plan of merger or adopt a plan of consolidation with another corporation;

d) Authorize the sale, lease, exchange or mortgage of all or substantially all of the property and assets of the BWA;

e) Authorize the voluntary dissolution of the BWA or revoke proceedings therefore;

f) Adopt a plan for the distribution of the assets of the BWA; or

g) Amend, alter or repeal any resolution of the Executive Committee which by its terms provides that it shall not be amended, altered or repealed by the committee.

3. BUDGET AND FINANCE COMMITTEE

The Budget and Finance Committee will assist the Executive Committee in overseeing the financial affairs of the BWA. The committee shall oversee:

(a) the operating and capital budgets;

(b) fiscal and investment policies and performance;

(c) other financial planning responsibilities as appropriate.

4. AUDIT COMMITTEE

The Audit Committee will assist the Executive Committee in overseeing audit related matters including the annual external audit of the BWA.

5. HUMAN RESOURCES COMMITTEE

The Human Resources Committee will assist the Executive Committee in overseeing matters relating to human resources. The committee will provide advice and counsel to the Executive Committee on matters relating to personnel and benefits, and oversee the development of appropriate human resources policies and procedures including a comprehensive personnel handbook.

6. MEMBERSHIP COMMITTEE

The Membership Committee will assist the Executive Committee in overseeing matters relating to membership of the BWA. The Committee will review applications for membership and associate membership of the BWA, consulting, as appropriate, with the relevant region of the BWA.

7. BAPTIST WORLD AID COMMITTEE

The Baptist World Aid Committee will assist the Executive Committee in overseeing matters relating to the Baptist World Aid programs of the BWA which promote relief and sustainable development.

8. THE BAPTIST WORLD CONGRESS COMMITTEE

The Baptist World Congress Committee will assist the Executive Committee in overseeing matters relating to the planning and execution of the Baptist World Congresses.

ARTICLE VI
OFFICERS OF THE BWA

1. PRESIDENT

The President of the BWA is appointed for a quinquennium by the General Council upon nomination from the Nominations Committee. The President is affirmed by the Baptist World Congress. The President will normally preside over the Baptist World Congress and the General Council. In the absence of, or at the discretion of the President, the First Vice-President or one of the Vice-Presidents may be called upon to preside from time to time.

The President is expected to work cooperatively with the General Secretary and the Executive Committee for the effective implementation of the programs of the BWA. The President will perform such tasks as agreed in the Presidential Job Description adopted and revised from time to time by the General Council. The President is not a salaried officer of the BWA.

2. FIRST VICE PRESIDENT

The First Vice President is elected by the General Council on nomination from the Nominations Committee to serve as a deputy to the President for each Quinquennium. The First Vice President is expected to assist the President and work cooperatively with the General Secretary for the effective implementation of the programs of the BWA through such activities as fraternal counsel, messages, and visits to the constituency. The First Vice President is not a salaried officer of the BWA. Since the first Vice President is not a salaried officer, the BWA shall seek to assist the First Vice President with any necessary expense of specific work assignments from the President and General Secretary to the extent the budget permits. Assurance of reimbursement must be obtained in advance from the General Secretary.

3. VICE PRESIDENTS

Up to eleven other Vice Presidents are appointed for each Quinquennium by the General Council upon nomination from the Nominations Committee to promote and seek support for the work of the BWA. They are to undergird the Regional Fellowship or Federation in their respective areas and to carry out other responsibilities as requested by the General Council, the Executive Committee, the President, or the General Secretary. Since they are not salaried officers, the BWA shall seek to assist them with any necessary expense of specific work assignments from the President and General Secretary to the extent the budget permits. Assurance of reimbursement must be obtained in advance from the General Secretary. The Vice-Presidents are responsible for encouraging financial support for the BWA from the Member Bodies in their respective areas.

4. GENERAL SECRETARY

The General Secretary shall be the chief executive officer of the BWA. The General Secretary shall be accountable to the Executive Committee and shall in general supervise and control all of the business and affairs of the BWA. The General Secretary shall be primarily responsible for achieving the overall objectives of the BWA within the framework of policies and objectives approved by the Executive Committee, and within the delegated authority and responsibilities set forth in a job description developed and approved by the Executive Committee and confirmed by the General Council.

5. TREASURER

The Treasurer shall assist the General Secretary in overseeing the financial affairs of the BWA and causing to be kept and maintained adequate and comprehensive books and records of the assets and finances of the BWA. The Treasurer shall be a member of the Executive Committee. The Treasurer shall chair the Budget and Finance Committee of the Executive Committee. The Treasurer is not a salaried officer of the BWA.

ARTICLE VII
PATTERN OF WORK OF THE BWA

1. CLUSTERS OF COMMITMENT

Consistent with the Clusters of Commitment adopted by the General Council in 2007, the Executive Committee shall establish and oversee the pattern of work of the BWA, including the approval of executive staff positions necessary and appropriate to support such programs. Based on the approved Clusters of Commitment, the work of the BWA will focus on the following areas: worship and fellowship; mission and evangelism; religious liberty and human rights; relief and sustainable community development; and theological reflection.

2. COMMISSIONS

Commissions and Committees may be established from time to time by the Executive Committee, drawing together appropriate persons from Member Bodies to serve in reflection, study and, where appropriate, action. The Nominations Committee will receive, review and recommend persons to the General Council to serve as core members on such Commissions and

Committees. The scope of work and responsibilities of each Commission or Committee will be set forth in a charter approved by the Executive Committee.

ARTICLE VIII
REGIONAL FELLOWSHIPS OR FEDERATIONS

1. PURPOSE

a) The Regional Fellowships or Federations (hereinafter Regions) shall reflect the objectives of the BWA in their geographical regions and as such shall primarily be expressions of the BWA.

b) The respective Member Bodies may have direct membership in both the BWA and the Region. Membership in a region does not in any way limit the direct relationship with the BWA.

c) Regions shall normally be organized on a continental basis.

d) Regions should demonstrate continuing progress toward self-support.

2. RELATIONSHIPS

The BWA currently recognizes the following Regional Fellowships and Federations: All Africa Baptist Fellowship; Asia Pacific Baptist Federation; Caribbean Baptist Fellowship; European Baptist Federation; North American Baptist Fellowship; Union of Baptists of Latin America.

a) Each Member Body of the BWA is encouraged to affiliate with a Regional Fellowship or Federation. Upon approval of the BWA Executive Committee, a Member Body may be dually aligned with its own Regional Fellowship and one additional Fellowship for cultural and language reasons.

b) Each Region shall encourage all its member bodies to seek membership in the BWA. Prior to acceptance of new members, the BWA will consult with both the appropriate Region and the appropriate member body.

c) The General Council shall authorize the Region and agree on boundaries between the regions in consultation with the relevant regions.

d) The Regions shall be fully integrated into the life and structure of the BWA, but will elect their own officers and determine their own functions within the framework and policy of the BWA.

3. MEMBERSHIP OF OFFICERS

a) The President of the BWA shall be an ex officio member of all regional councils.

b) The Vice-Presidents of the BWA shall be ex officio members of the council or other representative body of their respective Regions.

4. EXECUTIVE STAFF AND REGIONAL STAFF

a) The General Secretary shall be an ex-officio member of all regional councils.

b) Regional secretaries will be responsible to their respective Region for the administration of its affairs, and to the General Secretary of the BWA as regional secretaries of the BWA.

c) The term of service as regional secretary shall coincide with service as executive officer of the Region.

d) Each Region shall appraise the work of its executive officer/regional secretary in consultation with the General Secretary of the BWA at least once in each Quinquennium.

5. FINANCES

a) Regional Fellowships may raise funds for their own regions but may not raise funds in the name of the BWA beyond their borders. The raising of such funds shall in no way obligate the BWA to any liability or obligation.

b) An annual application, including an annual budget, to the BWA for support of the work in the region should be submitted to the Executive Committee to be agreed for inclusion in the General Budget of the BWA.

c) An annual report shall be required of all income, expenditures, unpaid liabilities or obligations of each Region.

d) The books of each Region shall be audited annually and a copy of the report submitted to the BWA, not later than six months after the closing of the fiscal year of the Region.

6. REPORTS

Reports from each Region will be given at least twice a year to the General Secretary for presentation to the General Council and the Executive Committee. The reports should be received in writing by the General Secretary not later than six weeks prior to the respective meeting. The annual report should include membership statistics, notification of election results, progress of programs, reports of executive and council meetings and notification of future meetings.

ARTICLE IX
THE AUXILIARIES

1. The Executive Committee may, from time to time, authorize the establishment of auxiliaries of the BWA (hereinafter "Auxiliary"). The Auxiliaries currently authorized by the BWA include the following departments: men, women and youth.

2. Each Auxiliary shall develop bylaws which will be approved by the Executive Committee. The bylaws of each Auxiliary shall define the relationship between the Auxiliary and the BWA, as well as related regional organizations

3. An Auxiliary may elect a director upon recommendation of its own search committee and the General Secretary of the BWA. Each director

shall be responsible to the Auxiliary for the administration of its affairs and to the General Secretary as a member of the staff of the BWA.

Notwithstanding the provisions above, any Auxiliary staff employed by the BWA or whose salary is paid by the BWA in whole or in part, shall be appointed in accordance with and subject to the personnel policies and procedures of the BWA as approved by the Executive Committee. Such staff members will report directly to the General Secretary.

4. Officers of men, women, and youth work within a region shall be elected by members of the respective organizations and accepted by the regional body.

ARTICLE X
INDEMNIFICATION, INSURANCE & LIABILITY

1. INDEMNIFICATION

The BWA may, to the maximum extent allowed by law, indemnify any person who was or is a party or is threatened to be made a party to any threatened, pending, or completed action, suit, or proceeding, whether civil, criminal, administrative, or investigative, other than an action by or in the right of the BWA, by reason of the fact that he or she is or was a director, committee member, officer, employee, or agent of the BWA, or is or was serving at the request of the BWA as a director, officer, employee, or agent of another corporation, partnership, joint venture, trust, or other enterprise, against expenses, including attorneys' fees, judgments, fines, and amounts paid in settlement actually incurred by him or her in connection with such action, suit, or process. The amount of such indemnity shall be as much as the Executive Committee or the court, if application has been made to it, determines and finds to be reasonable.

2. INDEMNIFICATION EXCESS

The indemnity provided herein shall be in excess of all valid and collectible insurance or indemnity policies.

3. INSURANCE

The BWA shall purchase and maintain insurance on behalf of any individual who is or was a director, committee member, officer, or employee, of the BWA, or who, while a director, committee member, officer, or employee of the BWA, is or was serving at the request of the BWA as a director, officer, partner, trustee, or employee of another foreign or domestic business or nonprofit corporation, partnership, joint venture, trust, employee benefit plan, or other enterprise, against liability asserted against or incurred by him or her in that capacity or arising from his or her status as a director, committee member, officer, or employee, whether or not the BWA would have power to indemnify the person against the same liability under this Article of these Bylaws.

4. PERSONAL LIABILITY

Except as otherwise provided by law, no member of the Executive Committee or committees appointed by it, shall be personally liable, in his or her capacity as a committee member, for monetary damages for any action taken by such committee member or any failure by such committee member to take any action, unless the breach or failure to perform constitutes self-dealing, willful misconduct, or recklessness. This provision shall not apply to the responsibility or liability of a committee member pursuant to any criminal statute or the liability of a committee member for the payment of taxes pursuant to the laws applicable in the jurisdiction in which the BWA is registered.

ARTICLE XI
CONFLICT OF INTEREST

1. Each of the BWA's officers and Committee members (including the Executive Committee and committees appointed by it) (hereafter Committee members) shall act at all times in a manner that furthers the BWA's religious and charitable purposes and shall exercise care that he or she does not act in a manner that furthers his or her private interests to the detriment of the BWA's religious and charitable purposes. A conflict

of interest can be considered to exist in any instance where the actions or activities of an individual on behalf of the BWA also involve the obtaining of a direct or indirect personal gain or advantage, or an adverse or potentially adverse effect on the interests of the BWA. The BWA's officers and Committee members shall avoid conflicts of interest and otherwise fully disclose to the BWA any potential or actual conflicts of interest, if such conflicts cannot be avoided, so that such conflicts are dealt with in the best interests of the BWA.

2. The BWA and all of its officers and Committee members shall comply with any policies of the BWA regarding conflicts of interest, as well as all applicable legal requirements.

ARTICLE XII
RECORDS AND REPORTS

1. ARTICLES OF INCORPORATION AND BYLAWS

The BWA shall keep at its principal office a copy of its Articles of Incorporation and these Bylaws, as amended to date.

2. MAINTENANCE OF OTHER CORPORATE RECORDS

The BWA shall keep in written form correct and complete books and records of its accounts and shall also keep in written form minutes of the proceedings of the General Council, Executive Committee and any committees having any of the authority of the General Council or Executive Committee, and shall keep at the registered or principal office a record giving the names and addresses of the Executive Committee members.

3. CONFIDENTIALITY

Except as otherwise publicly disclosed, or in order to appropriately conduct the BWA's business, the records and reports of the BWA shall be held in confidence by those persons with access to them.

ARTICLE XIII
GENERAL PROVISIONS

1. FISCAL YEAR

The fiscal year of the BWA shall end on 31 December each year.

2. FISCAL POLICIES

The BWA shall develop such fiscal policies and procedures which are necessary and appropriate to meet applicable regulatory and audit requirements, and which will promote financial transparency and accountability for the BWA. All fiscal policies and procedures shall be approved by the Executive Committee upon recommendation of the Budget and Finance Committee. Fiscal policies and procedures shall include, but not be limited to the following areas: signatory authority relating to checks, indebtedness, contract and other legal obligations; approval of financial institutions for BWA accounts; investments; spending and gifts.

ARTICLE XIV
AMENDMENTS

1. AMENDMENTS

a) These Bylaws may be amended from time to time by the General Council, generally upon the recommendation of the Executive Committee as follows

a) If written notice of the meeting at which the amendments are presented is given to every member of the General Council at least three months in advance, and a quorum is present, then an affirmative vote of a simple majority of members present and voting shall be required for adoption.

b) If no advance written notice of the proposed bylaws amendments has been given, and a quorum is present, then an affirmative vote of a 4/5 majority of members present and voting shall be required for adoption.

2. REVIEW

The Bylaws will be periodically reviewed every five years during the second year of the Quinquennium.

22. Officers, Executive Staff & Regional Secretaries, 2010-2015

Officers

President	John Upton
General Secretary	Neville Callam
Treasurer	Carolyn Fossen
First Vice President	Daniel Carro
Vice Presidents	Regina Claas
	Ross Clifford
	Nabil Costa
	William Epps
	Harry Gardner
	Victor Samuel Gonzalez
	John Kok
	Olu Menjay
	Paul Msiza
	Joel Sierra
	Burchell Taylor

Elected Executive Staff

Raimundo Barreto	Freedom & Justice, Director
Pasty Davis	Women's Department, Director
Emmett Dunn	Youth Department and Conferences, Director
Forestal Lawton	Men's Department, Director
Paul Montacute	BWAid, Director
Fausto Vasconcelos	Mission, Evangelism & Theological Reflection, Director

Appointed Executive Staff

Eron Henry	Communications, Associate Director
Julie Justus	Executive Office, Member Services Manager
Meg Pearson	Finance, Comptroller
Kathe Traynham	Promotion & Development, Associate Director

Regional Secretaries

All Africa Baptist Fellowship	Harrison G. Olan'g
Asia Pacific Baptist Federation	Pushehu Bonny Resu
Caribbean Baptist Fellowship	Everton Jackson
European Baptist Federation	Tony Peck
Union of Baptists in Latin America	Alberto Prokopchuk
North American Baptist Fellowship	George Bullard

APPENDICES

APPENDIX I

PLENARY SPEAKERS

Alongla Aier is assistant professor of English and communication at Oriental Theological Seminary in Nagaland, India

Janet Clark is senior vice president (academic affairs), academic dean, and associate professor of counselling at Tyndale University College and Seminary in Toronto, Ontario, Canada

David Coffey was president of the Baptist World Alliance from 2005-2010

Pablo Deiros is president of the International Baptist Theological Seminary in Buenos Aires, Argentina

Allan Demond is senior pastor of New Hope Baptist Church in Melbourne, Australia

Karl Johnson is general secretary of the Jamaica Baptist Union

Paul Msiza is president of the All Africa Baptist Fellowship and general secretary of the South Africa Baptist Convention

Lance Watson is senior pastor of St. Paul's Baptist Church in Richmond, Virginia, USA

APPENDIX II

Language Bible Study Group Leaders

Alistair Brown: President, Northern Baptist Theological Seminary, Chicago, Illinois, USA

Daniel Carro: Professor of Divinity, John Leland Center for Theological Studies, Falls Church, Virginia, USA; First Vice President, BWA

Steve (Sekyu) Chang: Senior Pastor, Light Global Mission Church, Fairfax, Virginia, USA

Meilin Chen: Consultant, Crystal Cathedral and Hour of Power-International Ministry, California, USA

Wood-Ping Chu: General Secretary, Baptist Convention of Hong Kong; President, Asia Pacific Baptist Federation

Regina Claas: General Secretary, Union of Evangelical Free Churches in Germany; Vice President, BWA

Raquel Contreras: President, Union of Evangelical Baptist Churches, Chile; President, BWA Women's Department

Jonathan Edwards: General Secretary, Baptist Union of Great Britain

William Epps: Senior Pastor, Second Baptist Church, Los Angeles, California, USA; Vice President, BWA

Randel Everett: Executive Director, Baptist General Convention of Texas, USA

Adebola Fatokun: Administrator and Human Resources Practitioner, Lagos, Nigeria; Member, BWA Emerging Leaders Network

Samson Fatokun: Aviation Technocrat, International Air Transportation Association, Lagos, Nigeria; Member, BWA Emerging Leaders Network

Marlene Baltazar da Nóbrega Gomes: President, Latin American Baptist Women's Union; President, Woman's Missionary Union of Brazil

Volkmar Hamp: Chairman, European Baptist Federation Youth & Children Workers Conference

Myung Jim (Joseph) Ko: Senior Pastor, Suwon Central Baptist Church, Seoul, Korea

Shigemi Ono: Chairman, Japan Baptist Union Board; chair, Japan Baptist Overseas Mission Society; Professor, Japan Baptist Theological Seminary; Pastor, Itako Baptist Church

Emile Sam-Peale: Superintendent and Principal, Lott Carey Baptist Mission School, Browerville, Liberia

Peter Pinder: BWA Regional Secretary, Caribbean; Executive Secretary/ Treasurer, Caribbean Baptist Fellowship; Senior Pastor, Zion Baptist Church, Freeport, Bahamas

Alberto Prokopchuk: BWA Regional Secretary, Latin America; Executive Secretary, Union of Baptists in Latin America

Julie Pennington-Russell: Lead Pastor, First Baptist Church, Decatur, Georgia, USA

Jung Seung Ryong: Senior Pastor, Everlove Baptist Church, Daejeon, South Korea

Terry Smith: Director, Partnerships and Initiatives, Canadian Baptist Ministries; Adjunct Professor, Tyndale University College and Seminary; Adjunct Professor, Acadia Divinity College

Rachael Tan: Assistant Professor of Biblical Studies, Taiwan Baptist Theological Seminary; Associate Dean, Asia Baptist Graduate Theological Seminary; Member, BWA Emerging Leaders Network

Hikofumi Tomari: Pastor, Goya Baptist Church; Former Chair, Okinawa Baptist Convention

Fausto Vasconcelos: Director, Mission, Evangelism and Theological Reflection, BWA

Makito Watanabe: Japanese Language Pastor, Olivet Baptist Church, Honolulu, Hawai`i

APPENDIX III

Focus Group Moderators and Presenters

Nabeeh Abbassi: Past President, Jordan Baptist Convention

Koffi Adzam: Pastor, Trinity Baptist Church, London; Trustee, Baptist Union of Great Britain; Member, BWA Emerging Leaders Network

Denise Vasconcelos Araujo: Brazilian Youth Leader; President, BWA Youth Department; Member, BWA Emerging Leaders Network

Raimundo Barreto: Director, Freedom and Justice, BWA

John Beasy: National President, Australian Baptist Ministries

Jeremy Bell: Executive Minister, Baptist Union of Western Canada, Calgary

Rod Benson: Ethicist and Public Theologian, Tinsley Institute, Morling College, Sydney, Australia

Lauran Bethell: Global Consultant, International Ministries, American Baptist Churches USA; Human Rights Advocate; Recipient, 2005 BWA Quinquennial Human Rights Award

Cawley Bolt: Church Historian; President, Jamaica Baptist Union

Elijah Brown: Assistant Professor of Religion, East Texas Baptist University; Member, BWA Emerging Leaders Network

George Bullard: BWA Regional Secretary, North America; General Secretary, North American Baptist Fellowship; Ministry Colleague, Columbia Partnership, Columbia, South Carolina, USA

Karen Bullock: Professor, Christian Heritage, and Director, Ph.D. Program, B. H. Carroll Theological Institute, Arlington, Texas, USA

Jerry Carlisle: Senior Pastor, First Baptist Church, Plano, Texas, USA

Daniel Carro: Professor of Divinity, John Leland Center for Theological Studies, Falls Church, Virginia, USA; First Vice President, BWA

Joel Sierra Cavazos: Former Pastor, Monterey Baptist Church, Mexico; Pastor, First Baptist Church, Managua, Nicaragua; Vice President, BWA

Regina Claas: General Secretary, Union of Evangelical Free Churches in Germany; Vice President, BWA

Ross Clifford: Principal, Morling Seminary, Sydney, Australia; Vice President, BWA

Robert Cochran: Associate Executive Director and Staff Liaison, Center for Congregational Health, Evangelism & Discipleship, District of Columbia Baptist Convention, Washington, D.C., USA

Nabil Costa: Executive Director, Lebanese Society for Educational and Social Development; Vice President, BWA

Christer Daelander: Mission Secretary, Baptist Union of Sweden; Religious Freedom Coordinator, European Baptist Federation

Devon Dick: Pastor, Boulevard Baptist Church, St. Andrew, Jamaica; Adjunct Associate Professor of Nation Building, University of Technology, St. Andrew, Jamaica.

Han-ho Doh: President, Korea Baptist Theological University/Seminary, Daejon, Korea

Mauricio Droguett: Psychiatrist, Chile; Member, BWA Emerging Leaders Network

Deonie Duncan: Pastor, Buff Bay Circuit of Churches, Jamaica

Jonathan Edwards: General Secretary, Baptist Union of Great Britain

Wanne Garrey: Director, Relief and Development Department, Garo Baptist Convention of India; Member, BWA Emerging Leaders Network

David Goatley: Executive Secretary-Treasurer, Lott Carey Baptist Foreign Mission Convention, Washington, D.C., USA; President, North American Baptist Fellowship

Wilbert Goatley: Pastor, Calvary Missionary Baptist Church, Saint Louis, Missouri, USA

Brenda Harewood: Director, Pastoral Excellence Program, Lott Carey Baptist Foreign Mission Convention, USA

Johnathan Hemmings: Pastor, Ocho Rios Baptist Church, Jamaica

James Hill: Executive Director, Baptist General Convention of Missouri, USA

Johnny B. Hill: President, Foundation for Reconciliation and Dialogue; Senior Pastor, Greater Hope Baptist Church, Louisville, Kentucky, USA

Solomon Ishola: General Secretary, Nigerian Baptist Convention

James Jackson: Senior Pastor, Goodwin Memorial Baptist Church, Harrisburg, Pennsylvania, USA; Professor, Kutztown University, Pennsylvania, USA

David Kerrigan: General Director, BMS World Mission, United Kingdom

Blake Killingsworth: Historian; Assistant to the President, Dallas Baptist University; Member, BWA Emerging Leaders Network

Karen Kirlew: Pastor, St. Ann's Bay Baptist Church, Jamaica

John Kok: Senior Pastor, Kuala Lumpur Baptist Church, Kuala Lumpur, Malaysia; Vice President, BWA

Chris Liebrum: Director, Education/Discipleship Center, Baptist General Convention of Texas, USA

Helle Liht: Assistant to the General Secretary, European Baptist Federation; Coordinator, Environmental Network, European Baptist Federation

Johnson T. K. Lim: Thesis Director for Doctoral Students, Asia Baptist Graduate Theological Seminary, Singapore

Emmanuel McCall: Pastor (Retired), Fellowship Group Baptist Church, East Point, Georgia, USA; Adjunct Instructor, McAfee School of Theology, Mercer University, Atlanta, Georgia, USA

Roy Medley: General Secretary, American Baptist Churches, USA

Tom Mei: Senior Pastor, Broadmoor Baptist Church, Vancouver, Canada

Olu Menjay: President, Rick's Institute, Monrovia, Liberia; Vice President, BWA; Member, BWA Emerging Leaders Network

Peter Mihaere: Director, Tranzsend, New Zealand Baptists in Global Mission

Henry Mugabe: Principal/President, Baptist Theological Seminary of Zimbabwe, Gweru, Zimbabwe

Rob Nash: Coordinator, Global Missions, Cooperative Baptist Fellowship, Atlanta, Georgia, USA

Gary Nelson: Former General Secretary, Canadian Baptist Ministries; President and Chief Executive Officer, Tyndale University College and Seminary, Toronto, Canada

Harrison Olan'g: President, Mt. Meru University, Arusha, Tanzania; BWA Regional Secretary, Africa; General Secretary, All Africa Baptist Fellowship

Suzii Paynter: Director, Advocacy/Care Center, Baptist General Convention of Texas, USA

Tony Peck: BWA Regional Secretary, Europe; General Secretary, European Baptist Federation

Bonny Resu: BWA Regional Secretary, Asia; General Secretary, Asia Pacific Baptist Federation

Zhanuo Asha Sanchu: Director, Miqlat Ministry, Nagaland Baptist Church Council, Nagaland, India; Member, Emerging Leaders Network

Robert Sellers: Professor of Missions, Logsdon School of Theology, Hardin Simmons University, Abilene, Texas, USA

Warren Stewart: Senior Pastor, First Institutional Baptist Church, Phoenix, Arizona

Michael Stroope: Associate Professor of Christian Missions, George W. Truett Theological Seminary, Baylor University, Texas, USA

Burchell Taylor: Senior Pastor, Bethel Baptist Church, St. Andrew, Jamaica; Lecturer, United Theological College of the West Indies, St. Andrew, Jamaica; Vice President, BWA

Michael Taylor: Head of Department of Physics, University of the West Indies, Mona Campus, Jamaica; Member, BWA Emerging Leaders Network

Clayton Teague: Director, National Nanotechnology Coordination Office, USA

Ellen Teague: Former Director, Finance and Administration, BWA; Executive Director, District of Columbia Baptist Convention Foundation, Washington, D.C., USA

Bill Tillman: T.B. Mason Professor of Christian Ethics, Logsdon Seminary, Hardin-Simmons University, Abilene, Texas, USA

Vladimir Ubeivolc: Former Senior Pastor, Light to the World Evangelical Baptist Church, Chisinau, Moldova; Lecturer, College of Theology and Education, affiliated with the Union of Evangelical Baptist Churches, Moldova; Director, Beginning of Life

Fausto Vasconcelos: Director, Mission, Evangelism and Theological Reflection, BWA

Graham B. Walker: Professor of Theology and Associate Dean, McAfee School of Theology, Mercer University, Atlanta, Georgia, USA

William G. Wilson: President, Center for Congregational Health, Wake Forest University Baptist Medical Center, Winston Salem, North Carolina, USA

Brian Winslade: National Director, Australian Baptist Ministries

Naw Blooming Night Zan: Burmese Activist; Leader, Karen Women's Organization